AÉROSPATIALE/BAC
CONCORDE

First published in hardback in a larger format in 2010 as *Aérospatiale/BAC Concorde Owners' Workshop Manual* Reprinted 2010, 2012, 2015, 2017, 2018 This edition published in 2018

A catalogue record for this book is available from the British Library

ISBN 978 1 78521 576 6

Library of Congress control no. 2018948553

Published by Haynes Publishing, Sparkford, Yeovil, Somerset BA22 7JJ, UK Tel: 01963 440635 Int. tel: +44 1963 440635 Website: www.haynes.com

Haynes North America Inc. 859 Lawrence Drive, Newbury Park, California 91320, USA

Design and layout by James Robertson

Cover picture supplied by Getty Images, page 3 by Alamy.

Printed in Malaysia

Authors' note

This manual is very much a view from the hub of British Airways Concorde operations during the 1970s and 80s; those hectic years in which so much of the post Entry-Into-Service technical, operational and commercial development took place and the blueprint for supersonic civil flight was laid down.

It was a period of unique co-operation between manufacturer and operator – on both sides of the Channel. The factories' Product Support Groups were magnificent in their advice, analysis and development of techniques for both the hangar and the flightdeck.

While never a joint operation in the true sense – although it was discussed at one point – the two Concorde fleets had only minor differences in equipment and procedures. It would have been perfectly feasible for British and French crews to work together; in fact, Braniff's crews, during their brief Concorde adventure, did operate aircraft from both fleets.

Both operators began as publicly owned nationalised companies and both are able to dispel dogma-driven profit and loss myths. For example, it is a simple matter of record that Concorde's contribution to profit helped pave the way to BA's flotation on the Stock Market.

Acknowledgements

Ian Black, former RAF fighter pilot, now an A340 Captain, for his kind permission to reproduce photographs; Allan Burney; Peter R. March/PRM Aviation; the Press Association; TopFoto; Oliver Dearden of the Bristol Aero Collection, Elizabeth Corsie and Andrew Treweek of the Concorde at Filton organisation for very kindly giving us full access to photograph Alpha Foxtrot; Dr Geoff Rowlands of Farnborough Air Sciences Trust; Senior Engineer Officers John Lidiard and Pete Phillips; Captain Roger Mills; John Dunlevy and Carl Percey, Concorde ground engineers; Capt Mike Bannister, Senior Engineer Officer Ian Smith and Gordon Roxborough for allowing us to use the Concorde flight simulator at Brooklands; specialist photography by Piers Macdonald Photography; Jonathan Falconer for his guidance throughout the project.

AÉROSPATIALE/BAC
CONCORDE

David Leney and David Macdonald

HAYNES **ICONS**

Contents

Chapter 1

The Concorde Story

Concorde, the world's first – the world's only – supersonic airliner. Conceived in the cauldron of imagination that was the 1950s and born into the 60s. Graduating from the aviation centres at Bristol and Toulouse, the bright lights of London, Paris and New York beckoned. That was the plan.

That over three hundred additional destinations joined in the supersonic adventure was no small surprise. From New Zealand to The Arctic Circle and at every point of longitude the echoes remain.

OPPOSITE Concorde prototypes 002 and 001 flank the pre-production 101 at the Fairford Flight Test Centre on 6 January 1972. Note the different visor configurations of the two prototypes and 101. *Farnborough Air Sciences Trust (FAST)*

Genesis

In civil aviation terms, history will look back on the latter half of the 20th century with some envy. From post-war DC-3s and Constellations to today's ubiquitous twin-jets, via 'jet-setting sixties' (707s and VC10s) and wide-bodied mass travel jumbos, it had been a hotbed of innovation.

And then there was Concorde, fourteen airliners that bestrode the era. A paradox; at once an integral part of those fertile years and yet, quite separate.

It was in 1954 that a group of chaps at the Royal Aircraft Establishments (RAE) of Bedford and Farnborough began to consider the feasibility of a supersonic airliner. Such a simple sentence to read, but consider 1954. To fly any distance, the choice would have been Lockheed Constellation, Boeing Stratocruiser, Douglas DC-6 or the recently introduced DC-7. More significantly, the first passenger jet 'plane, Britain's de Havilland Comet 1, had just been grounded – permanently, following a series of accidents and structural failures during its two years of operation. The first successful jets, Comet 4 and Boeing 707 were still four years away: the Comet, very much a 1950s aircraft,

while the 707, through many models, would evolve into a fine aircraft.

Against this backdrop, to suggest a jet-powered (a must) supersonic airliner was bold, verging on the outrageous, yet the building blocks were there. The Cold War need for high-performance, high-speed fighters had driven aerodynamic research towards the right sort of wing, while the V-bomber programme (Valiant, Victor and Vulcan) had produced an engine with development potential.

In 1954 the Bristol Olympus engine, earmarked for military applications, had achieved 11,000lbs thrust. One of your authors would hang around aircraft at Renfrew airfield and the other was undergoing pilot training in the RAF.

By 1956 the omens were good. RAE reported positively to government, recommending that UK industry take the project forward, and so, on 1 October 1956 the Supersonic Transport Aircraft Committee (STAC) was born, chaired by Morien Morgan, then Deputy Director of RAE. Its brief, to institute a programme of research and design leading to a viable Supersonic Transport – the SST was conceived!

BELOW The British prototype Concorde 002 overflies Farnborough in the early 1970s. *FAST*

In an unprecedented peace-time spirit of co-operation, pretty well every British aircraft and aero-engine manufacturer took part.

STAC's work was completed in April 1959; it had been thorough and all-encompassing. The bottom line recommendations were that the UK should proceed with all urgency to build a transatlantic range aircraft to fly at not less than Mach 1.8 (1,200mph) and at the same time consider a smaller, medium range aircraft to cruise at Mach 1.2 (800mph). Such a dossier must have been hot property and indeed it was classified immediately as restricted to approved parties, UK only. This was not a document for international sharing. Or was it?

By 1959 Bristol Engines had merged with Armstrong Siddeley to become Bristol Siddeley Engines Ltd (BSEL): the Olympus was the engine of choice for the Avro Vulcan bomber and had achieved 17,000lbs thrust. One of the authors was now a BOAC pilot and the other a fourth-year apprentice with British European Airways.

Straightaway the Ministry of Aviation invited tenders from industry. Gone was the altruism of STAC, for now it was company against company, but not quite country against country. Even with the dossier still under lock and key, there appeared to be just a suggestion that it might be prudent to share costs. The USA were no good, they were playing with Mach 3 and in 1960 everyone knew that that was too much too soon; Germany wasn't interested, but in France Sud Aviation of Toulouse were doing something rather similar – a medium range (2,000 miles), 70-seat SST powered by four Rolls-Royce RB167 engines – it was a slender delta.

Hawker Siddeley and the Bristol Aeroplane Co (not yet BAC) bid for the contract. Bristols got the nod with a 198 model – long range, 130 seats, 380,000lbs maximum weight and six Olympus engines – a slender delta. At this time it was strictly drawing board. Worries about cost, complexity and sonic boom saw the 198 morph into the Bristol 223 – smaller, 100 seats, 250,000lbs maximum weight and four Olympus engines – it was a slender delta, too.

Bristol merged with Vickers and English Electric to form the British Aircraft Corporation

(BAC) in 1960; they invited Sud Aviation over for the weekend, getting on really well – lots of things in common, particularly slender deltas! Sud still planned medium range and BAC long, but the economy of same wing, body and engine design found favour in both camps (think Airbus A320 family, from A318 to A321). On 8 June 1961 an engagement was announced as BAC and Sud met to discuss formally, for the first time, a common design.

Interestingly, Sir Arnold Hall, who was Director RAE in 1954 when the SST debate was launched, was by 1958 the Managing Director of BSEL. Pre-empting Anglo/French aircraft co-operation he concluded that partnership was the only way such a project could work and by 1961 had established a joint venture with SNECMA the French engine company. They were ready and waiting.

In December 1961 the French and British governments came on board, after all they were the ones who would spend our money on the project. For most of 1962 technical and financial details were hammered out. By October it was agreed that France would be responsible for a medium range aircraft, 2,700 miles, 220,000lbs maximum weight; and UK the long range 3,700 miles, 270,000lbs maximum weight.

Both would be Mach 2.2, 100-passenger aircraft powered by four Olympus engines. Apart from a ventral door in the French aircraft, the only major difference would be fuel capacity; essentially they were each a variant of the same design.

Finally, the great day arrived, 29 November 1962. France and Britain signed an agreement to develop and build an SST; there was no escape clause. A marriage had taken place.

By 1962 BSEL had merged with Rolls-Royce, henceforth all references would be to the Rolls-Royce Olympus – now in its 593D evolution. Suffix 'D' denoted an engine derived from the TSR2 unit, now with reheat and a variable nozzle and 28,800lbs of thrust.

One author had now become a Senior First Officer on the Bristol Britannia 'Whispering Giant', the other fledged from the BOAC Flight Engineer school and ensconced on the de Havilland Comet 4.

Against huge odds and despite political vacillations an aircraft was produced. Without an international partnership and two industry-building design centres it might not have been so. The meticulous, step-by-step programme of research and test culminated in a Mach 2 airliner that brought the possibility of supersonic flight to all air travellers.

By the end of 1975 the Olympus 593-610 was certificated, at 32,080lbs of thrust. Concorde was awarded a full Certificate of Airworthiness by France and Britain.

One author was about to relinquish his position of Flight Manager VC10s to become Concorde Project Pilot, later Manager, while the other joined the fleet as a Flight Engineer Superintendent.

An engineering challenge

November 1962 was the watershed, when soaring imaginations met pragmatism. It was time to draw not a concept but an aircraft, to specify not such materials as may be useful but those that would be used, to plan not a fleeting visit to the Sound Barrier but a life beyond. Intellectual exercise had become engineering challenge.

STAC's work, and legacy to industry, pointed to a slender delta wing, Mach 2 and a need to work in a fourth dimension; not 'time', but 'temperature'. At twice the speed of sound skin temperature would rise to +130°C. Every facet of design would begin with that thought. For structure a special aluminium alloy would be used. Speeds above Mach 2.2 were discarded quickly; that was stainless steel and titanium territory.

The seven Articles of Agreement specified BAC/Sud as the chosen companies, giving them the responsibility to make proposals on both medium and long range aircraft, with equal share collaboration. A standing committee of officials would supervise the project on behalf of the two governments.

As the new organisation got to work in 1963 the long range aircraft was drawn at 280,000lbs take-off weight (TOW). BOAC, Air France and Pan Am all took out options to purchase, while across the ocean President Kennedy announced funding for an American SST, inviting tenders for design. Meanwhile,

BELOW 001, F-WTSS, the French-assembled prototype of the Anglo-French supersonic airliner, made her official public debut at Toulouse on 11 December 1967. *Barratt's/PA Photos/ EMP.4557066*

President de Gaulle had been heard to describe the European project as 'Concorde'. And so it became, although it wasn't until December 1967 that UK agreed to the 'e' at the end.

By 1964, amidst some acrimony, the medium range option was dropped and the long range version enlarged to 335,000lbs TOW with space for 100 passengers, from the pre-production aircraft onwards. It had been decided that flight-test would be conducted by two prototypes, two pre-prod, and two 'production aircraft'.

Generally speaking at this stage of an aircraft's gestation a company would stop drawing and start building a test prototype that would closely resemble the final production spec: it would use industry-accrued knowledge plus latest ideas to evolve its newest product. For Concorde there was no accrued knowledge, so when, in1965, the factories began building-up parts for 001 and 002 there was no design freeze, no diminution of research effort, it was a continuous production line of innovations and ideas, right up to the 'B' model.

In 1967 a substantial redefinition of the pre-prod aircraft brought TOW up to 367,000lbs and potential passengers to 130. Revised wing tips

and leading edges and extended rear fuselage would reduce drag: extra tankage and a new nose shape with fully glazed visor completed the package. On 11 December that year Concorde met her public for the first time when 001 was rolled-out from the Toulouse hangar.

First flights

By agreement, 001, F-WTSS, made the first flight on 2 March 1969, flown by André Turcat, Co-pilot Jacques Guignard, Flight Engineer Michel Retif and Henri Perrier leading the Flight Test Engineer team. It was a 42-minute flight at 10,000ft, 250kts from Toulouse to Toulouse. Five weeks later on 9 April, 002, G-BSST, made her maiden flight from Filton to Fairford, flown by Brian Trubshaw, Co-pilot John Cochrane, Flight Engineer Brian Watts with John Allen leading the Flight Test Engineers. Coincidentally, this flight was also 42 minutes, but this time at 8,000ft and 280kts.

Of the testing years ahead, André Turcat was quoted: 'Rate of progress will be dictated by prudence. We are entering a new realm, not by sudden breakthrough, but by efficient and careful exploration.'

BELOW The very first flight-test crew, Toulouse, 2 March 1969. From left to right: Chief Test Pilot André Turcat, Test Pilot Jean Guignard, and Flight Engineers Henri Perrier and Michel Retif. *PA Photos/EMP.2610008*

ABOVE Bell X1 rocket-propelled aircraft.
PRM Aviation

The Sound Barrier

Part 1 – The atmosphere

Fact – the speed at which sound travels through the air has a finite value. Watch a chap at the end of the road wield a hammer; see the hammer strike; it's almost a second later that the noise is heard. Thunder is created at the same time as its flash of lightning: observe the lightning, its image arrives 'instantaneously', count the seconds until thunder is heard, then divide those seconds by five to find how far away, in miles, the lightning struck. Sound is a pressure wave; all pressure waves through air behave like this.

Fact – the speed at which sound travels through the air is not a fixed value, it varies with temperature: the higher the temperature, the faster sound travels, or, to express it differently, the higher the speed of sound. Hence, in the 1950s, airspeed record attempts took place in hot regions, where aircraft could reach high speed without encountering the 'Sound Barrier'.

A brief word on atmospheric temperature. The sun heats the Earth, which warms the atmosphere, thus the further we are from the Earth's surface, the colder it gets.

Fact – if it's behaving itself, atmospheric temperature reduces at the rate of 1.9° Centigrade for each 1,000ft climbed – the Lapse Rate. But the atmosphere is a funny old thing. While flying across the North Atlantic, cruise-climbing between 50,000 and 60,000ft, the air temperature would have been about -55°C, while on the run down to Barbados, through the tropics, it became –75 to –80°C. Why? The Lapse Rate is only true up to a certain height, and this height is a variable. It is called the tropopause and across our North Atlantic region it is found at about 36,000ft, but in the tropics it can be up to 50,000ft.

Part 2 – Flying in it

When a 'plane makes a movement or disturbance in the air, warning of that movement transmits, via air molecules, to some 100 yards or so ahead, as a pressure wave. Thus warned, the air stream can divide neatly, to flow over and under the wing in an orderly manner. That pressure wave travelled at the (local) speed of sound. The airflow behaved rather like a liquid – it wasn't compressed in any sort of way. At this stage, 'compressibility' is introduced. Think of a bicycle pump – fill the chamber with water, block the outlet, then try to depress

the handle: the water cannot be compressed, cannot be squeezed into a smaller volume as could air. Air is a gas, it is able to be 'compressed'. Until aircraft began to approach the speed of sound, compressibility could be ignored; air flowed over the wing and round the aircraft and everything was fine, because of the warning waves travelling ahead at the speed of sound.

Then one day, perhaps through sheer exuberance in a dive, an aircraft came close to the speed of sound. Consider all those warning waves trying to go about their business, but now a brute of an aircraft is travelling at the same speed, right at their backside. There is no pre-warning. The first the air knows about the approaching machine is – wham! Then wham again and again etc. Instead of an orderly flow generating lift, the air piles up and because it is a gas, because it's 'compressible', it forms a bit of a pressure wave. Aerodynamic people call it a 'shock wave', which from the air's point of view is not a bad name.

The above is an obvious simplification to lead the reader towards the shock wave. A subsonic designer will steer clear of them. A supersonic designer knows from the start that he must work with them and so does the power plant designer.

Shock waves can, and do, form before an aircraft gets to the speed of sound: it's the airflow speeding-up over the curvy upper surface of the wing. The thicker the wing, the earlier this phenomenon will occur. The dear old Spitfire from the Second World War, although not designed to fly anywhere near the speed of sound, could achieve almost Mach 0.9, 9/10 of sonic speed before shock waves developed – because of its thin wing. Post-war, it was used to research what had become known popularly as the 'Sound Barrier'. A point now defined as an abrupt increase in drag, an equally sudden loss of lift, pressure distribution above and below the wing in a state of flux, turbulent flow behind the shocks and an aircraft now becomes unstable.

In following chapters we will see how aircraft designers blew the sound barrier apart, leaving only the 'Transonic Region' to pick one's way through. It is now considered as an area of high drag, an area where wings become less efficient at lifting. But proceed further, say beyond Mach 1.4 and drag reduces, wings recover efficiency, order returns, but the rules have changed. We will see how designers got to grips with these changes and how some learned to love them.

ABOVE An English Electric Lightning approaches the sound barrier. Low pressure above the wings causes a condensation cloud, with a shock wave forming behind. *PRM Aviation*

The apparent hiatus over most of 1970 was totally filled with transonic and systems work and tuning and modifying the Intake Control System in readiness for the final push to Mach 2 and 60,000ft, as soon as the -3B engines became available. Up to Mach 1.5 all flights had been made with fixed intakes. For the record, the first supersonic flight was conducted by 001 on 1 October 1969 after 115 hours of test flying. During a 1 hour 51 minutes flight to the north of Toulouse the aircraft reached 36,000ft and flew at Mach 1.05 for 9 minutes.

Flight-testing

A written summary of Concorde's flight-test schedules would appear similar to those for a subsonic aircraft – flutter, stability, handling, performance, engines, systems, limits, simulated failures etc., but the super-thin wing, long slender body and a supersonic aircraft of such size changed everything. As a statement of intent, in 1969, the Joint Company announced: 'The critical path to progress to Mach 2 is through the realms of intake geometry and flutter testing'. When an aircraft meets turbulence or a gust, the whole structure must damp-out any deflection or flexing, without pilot or system intervention: it must not be provoked into continuous vibration or oscillation at its natural frequency. That would be 'flutter'.

Such tests, beginning in June 1969, were conducted at many combinations of altitude, airspeed and mach no. in preparation for Mach 1, then continued through the minefield that is the transonic zone (about 0.98 to 1.4) where drag is dominant and lift struggles. They were repeated in 1972 throughout the flight envelope by the larger and heavier pre-production aircraft and once again to verify the final version when structure was strengthened to cope with TOW growth to 408,000lbs.

The mechanism of flutter testing was threefold. Entry level would be the 'stick jerk' whereby a momentary abrupt input to the flight controls is made. Slightly more complex would be a calibrated, electrically induced, wobble to the controls; finally, a small explosive charge would be attached to a control surface and actually detonated in flight, these were called 'bonkers'. It is left to the reader's imagination as to which definition of the word to use.

In all cases the aircraft would displace from steady flight, in pitch roll or yaw, depending on the test, and would return, or not, to stability. In common with most testing, everything was recorded for subsequent analysis. Concorde's structure and aerodynamic response provided good damping throughout the envelope.

André Turcat again: 'This system of variable geometry intake is really the big new feature of our aircraft, more so than the delta wing form or the flying control system.'

The testing years warrant a volume of their own. Only a taster is possible here, though intakes were in fact a main course. Here is a brief summary:

The variable geometry intake

'For the first four months of flight nothing on the intake moved. In July 1969 the precursor to the Spill Door was fitted to the intake floor (*see Chapter 3: The Power to Move*); known as the 'barn door,' it had a hinge at each end. Above Mach 0.7 it was hinged at the front and acted just like a spill door, but at low speeds a change-over mechanism engaged a rear hinge and disconnected the front so that it could be lowered as a forward-

facing auxiliary inlet scoop. It was a worry: it was morphed into the Spill Door from pre-prod onward. By the mid-1970s the control system was fully operative, in analogue form, and speeds were extended towards Mach 2, albeit with much adjustment and tuning. TSS Rules, the standards written for Concorde, state, inter alia, that the operation must remain surge free throughout the envelope: testing and demonstrating that point was major, major work. In January 1971 a good old bang (a sympathetic surge in fact) blew the front ramp right off – more redesign, more tests. At the end of 1971 the wing leading edge profile was changed again – this time to prevent

ABOVE On the closing night of the Paris Air Show on 8 June 1969, the crowd saw 002 fly across Le Bourget airfield as 001 was about to take off. Note the rear fuselage speed brakes deployed on the upper Concorde. *Aérospatiale*

BELOW Concorde static test rig at RAE Farnborough, 1973. *FAST*

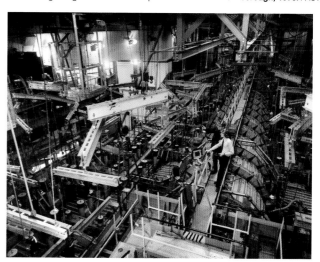

Tupolev Tu-144 – 'Concordski'

Alexei Andreivitch Tupolev's Tu-144 supersonic airliner is right up there alongside, 'who shot JFK?' and the moon landing, when it comes to conspiracy theories. While it is true that the USSR have built some derivative aircraft, when it comes to sustained Mach 2 flight, Bristol, Handley Page, Hawker-Siddeley, BAC, Sud-Aviation, Nord Aviation, Dassault, Aérospatiale, Lockheed, McDonnell Douglas, NASA and, after a flirtation with swing wing, Boeing, all drew slender deltas. It was no surprise then that Alexei and his company-founder father, Andrei, did likewise. When aerodynamics, strength, fuel and payload are considered, some version of the slender delta was the only viable choice.

The two SSTs, Concorde and Tu-144, were developed pretty much in parallel. USSR began talks in 1959, initiated design studies in 1961 and announced the project in 1962, the year of the Anglo/French agreement.

The 144's development content was quite staggering, due in no small part to the fundamental design changes made. Power plant location was moved outboard, possibly looking for best aerodynamic position and least adverse wing flow interference: this in itself necessitated a complete rethink on main landing gear design and location. Three different engines were tried, a Kuznetsov turbojet, same company's bypass engine and finally a Kolesov turbojet; each one would have required a re-matching of intakes and nozzles. Only the last-named engine was capable of supporting supercruise without reheat.

And then the wing; initially it was a variation of the curved ogival shape, but lacking the subtleties of camber and twist found on Concorde. While performing reasonably at high speed, its low speed handling required a fast approach and touchdown. Couple this with a lack of thrust reverse and clearly something had to be done; braking parachutes are fine for test, but not production. During Concorde's development there were changes to leading-edge profile and to outer wing shape, but these were as nothing compared to the production 144's new, angular double-delta (a reduction in sweep-back from about half way along the leading edge) and retractable fore planes. The wing itself was more sophisticated, more capable throughout the flight envelope. Fore planes were extended for low speed flight. They produced lift in their own right; therefore trimming the aircraft – to fly hands off – required some 'down elevon', which would act in the same way as flap on a subsonic – allowing a lower approach speed.

It is readily acknowledged that the 144's test programme began with a flight on 31 December 1969 (Concorde 2 March 1969); she was first through the sound barrier on 5 June 1969 (1 October 1969) and first to Mach 2 in May 1970 – probably the 26th – (Concorde 4 November 1970). Even the coveted supersonic entry-into-service accolade fell to the 144 (Moscow to Alma Ata on 26 December 1976), but it is generally accepted that this date marked only the beginning of cargo services. It took until 1 November 1977 – the 60th anniversary of the Bolshevik October uprising (there is a one month difference between the Julian and Gregorian calendars) – before the aircraft was deemed ready for passengers.

Range was restricted to approximately 2,500 miles due to the continuous use of reheat to maintain speed, thus precluding overseas destinations. After 55 flights, reliability issues forced a withdrawal from service.

BELOW Tupolev Tu-144, the first production 'S' model.
Novosti/TopFoto RIA07-010805

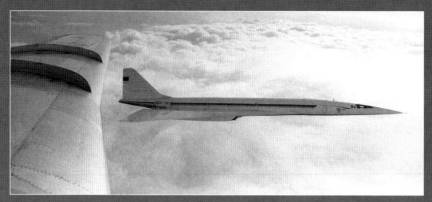

LEFT Tu-144 in flight. Note the nose profile similarity to the prototype Concorde. *Novosti/TopFoto RIA06-016757*

At the Paris Air Show on 3 June 1973, the development programme suffered severely when the first production model Tu-144S (registration 77102) crashed during a demonstration flight. The aircraft underwent a violent nose-down manoeuvre and while attempting a recovery from the consequent dive, it broke up and fell to the ground, destroying 15 houses, killing 8 occupants, and all 6 crew members on board. The cause of the accident, whether an overnight change to the aircraft's flight controls or interference from a French Mirage aircraft, remains controversial to this day.

The radically altered 'D' model, with more efficient engines and increased range, began a short-lived series of cargo services followed by a programme of upper atmospheric research during the 1980s. The last aircraft to be built, 'D' model 77114, was revived and overhauled in 1998–99, and was then contracted to USA's National Aeronautics and Space Administration (NASA) to provide training for shuttle pilots and research into the USA's High Speed Civil Transport version 2. It is interesting to note that in addition to NASA's Langley and Dryden centres, Boeing, Pratt & Whitney and General Electric were all beneficiaries of this government research programme.

In all, 16 Tu-144s were built: 2 prototypes, 9 144S and 5 144D production models. So much was achieved; it may only have been the final few aerodynamic and control refinements that eluded the Tupolev dynasty.

Tu-144 Facts

- First flight 31 December 1968.
- First flight above Mach 1, 5 June 1969.
- First flight above Mach 2, 26 May 1970.
- In the aviation world the Tu-144 is never referred to as 'Concordski'.

BELOW LEFT A Tu-144 'D' model in low speed flight, landing gear down, nose down and canards extended. *PRM Aviation*

BELOW One way to dry a runway! Tu-144S, 77102, lifts off at the Paris Air Show on 3 June 1973. She crashed minutes later. *Flight Collection/ TopFoto FLC006740*

vortex ingestion that led to...surge. High speed negative 'g' and sideslip also created flow distortion that led to...surge.

Test Pilot Gilbert Defer, 'It has taken us two years of modifications and careful flight-test to establish safety (freedom from surge) in the case of pushover (-ve 'g') and suddenly applied sideslip above Mach 1.'

Control stability was eased and certification gained when, late in the game, the analogue system was dropped in favour of the BAC Guided Weapons Division's digital control – the first civil use of such circuitry.

First Mach 2 flight was planned for 002 on 4 November 1970. Unfortunately during acceleration a hot gas leak triggered a fire warning on No. 2 engine, necessitating a shut-down and return to base. With 001 ready and waiting the French crew went into the record book that same afternoon. In a flight of 2hrs 16min, 1.16 was supersonic with 53min at Mach 2. Aircraft 001 followed on 12 November with a 2.26 flight including 1.19 supersonic of which 51min was at Mach 2.

Flight-test was rounded off across the summer of 1975 with a three-month 'Endurance Flying' programme. The authorities required 750 hours, flying a typical route network with airline participation; invited guests masqueraded as passengers.

Olympus Type Approval granted on 29 September 1975.
French Certificate of Airworthiness (C-of-A) awarded on 9 October 1975.
British C-of-A was withheld until 5 December 1975, due to an autopilot dispute between BA and BAC.

The year 1975 ended in a flurry of activity as the emphasis now swung towards the airlines. Ops manuals were brought up to date with the aircraft's final standard; procedures evolved during summer flying, were published and practised on simulators – and then the business of buying an aircraft – buying a Concorde.

A bitter sweet occasion, this the pinnacle of achievement for the manufacturers – certification of the Concorde variants 191,101 and 102 as airliners, tempered by the knowledge that each factory would build only seven; there would be no 'B' model, no improved Olympus.

There will never be such a ground breaking team in aviation again – ever. They are saluted.

At each purchase the men and women of Bristol came out to watch, knowing that their fledgling would turn once more for home runway, wheels up, maximum speed, height undisclosed – a blur of sound and emotion!

Naturally by EIS the aircraft was technically and operationally complete, a fully certificated airliner, and nothing described henceforth detracts from the rigour of design and build or from the thoroughness of verification. In fact Brian Trubshaw in his book, *Concorde: The Inside Story*, is of the opinion, 'the real problems with a new aircraft always seem to occur after it is finally placed in the hands of the airline operator'.

In short, the challenge had shifted from 'how do we get to Mach 2 at 60,000ft', to 'how can we live there?' The baton was passed.

BELOW Concorde 102, F-WTSA, carried the liveries of both Air France and British Airways and was used extensively in the flight development and certification programmes. She is pictured at Fairbanks, Alaska, in February 1974 undergoing cold weather trials.
Airbus UK

ABOVE **Work
progresses at Filton
on three production
Concordes for British
Airways, including
G-BOAC in mid-
ground.** *Airbus UK*

Conspiring against an easy transition were the twin nemeses of temperature and vibration. 'A total temperature of +127°C' is a Concorde phrase, once exotic, now commonplace, perhaps dulled by use. That one could sip champagne, or tea, at Mach 2 lent an air of normality – that was the plan. But there was a piece of bare frame in the flight deck too hot to maintain touch, rain water trapped inside cockpit double-glazing was seen to boil at Mach 1.8 – gone by Mach 2 and on one occasion the collapse of the flight deck cooling duct (–10°C inside) rendered M2 flight untenable. It was not going to be an easy ride.

Boldness and ingenuity had been tested in laboratories, workshops, hangars and cockpits, now they were to be examined in the market place. It all began on 21 January 1976 with BA's inaugural London–Bahrain supersonic passenger service using Concorde G-BOAA; and Air France's inaugural supersonic service from Paris to Rio de Janeiro via Dakar, with F-BVFA.

At 11.16am precisely, John Lidiard pushed the button and called, 'starting 3'. At 11.20am Captain Norman Todd, at London-Heathrow, exchanged fraternal greetings with Pierre Dudal in Paris and at 11.40am, to the second, Speedbird 300 and Air France 085 took to the air on the world's inaugural supersonic passenger flights.

Bahrain was only the first leg of the proposed route to Australia, via Singapore. The journey was expected to take Concorde 13½ hours. A settlement with Singapore in 1977 brought that station on-line, only to be followed by a 13-month hiatus as Malaysia extracted its due. With Indian, Indonesian and Australian negotiations ahead and increasing hostilities in the Middle East, a scheduled supersonic Eastern route became completely untenable and was abandoned in October 1980. Later, ad hoc charters across the region became a regular addition to Concorde's portfolio.

At Bristol and Toulouse it was straight back to work on changes and improvements. There were three items of major significance crystallised during the 'endurance flying' segment of 1975 testing:

- The main landing gear damping arrangement had to be altered to minimise vertical and lateral oscillations of the forward fuselage during take-off from undulating runways.
- Rapid temperature changes during supercruise in the tropics led to substantial Mach number excursions.
- A redesign of autopilot cruise modes and a linking to auto throttle provided the answer.
- The Olympus combustion chamber underwent several stages of improvement before being completely redesigned. Deliveries began in 1981.

An early performance improvement proposal concerned 'Contingency Rating' – the limited

John Lidiard – flight engineer, Concorde G-BOAA, 21 January 1976

When operating as a BOAC flight engineer on a Lockheed Constellation into Bahrain in 1955, little did I realise that some twenty years later on 21 January 1976 I would be the flight engineer with British Airways on the inaugural flight of Concorde, the world's first supersonic passenger aircraft, flying into Bahrain.

The atmosphere at Heathrow Airport on the day of the inaugural flight was electric, with spectators all around the airport and crammed onto the top of the Queen's Building. Having spent time with Captains Norman Todd and Brian Calvert at the pre-flight briefing discussing the route, fuel requirements and weather, I went to the aircraft to check the refuelling. I then did an external check of the aircraft before joining the captains on the flight deck to carry out pre-flight checks prior to start-up.

The passenger list was a mixture of fare-payers who had booked their seats years before, special guests, VIPs and the Press, who would be filming and broadcasting during the flight.

Two engines were started and the aircraft was pushed back from the stand. The other two engines were then started and everything worked perfectly. We taxied out to Runway 28L where we had a slight wait to ensure that the Air France Concorde at Paris-Charles de Gaulle Airport was in an identical position, as both Concordes would be making a synchronised take-off to be shown to the world on television.

The take-off went according to plan and the subsonic flight across Europe was uneventful. The small flight deck had a never ending stream of interested passengers. Once over the Adriatic and south of Venice the aircraft was accelerated to supersonic speed. This stage of the flight gave me more systems to monitor as the power plant intakes were now operating. I had to transfer fuel aft in order to keep the aircraft centre of gravity in the correct position and also ensure the aircraft was trimmed correctly for optimum supersonic cruise.

We flew over the Mediterranean, south of Crete then Cyprus, north of Beirut across

BELOW G-BOAA flew the first British Airways Concorde commercial service on 21 January 1976. Here she is being prepared for the inaugural service.
Arthur Kemsley

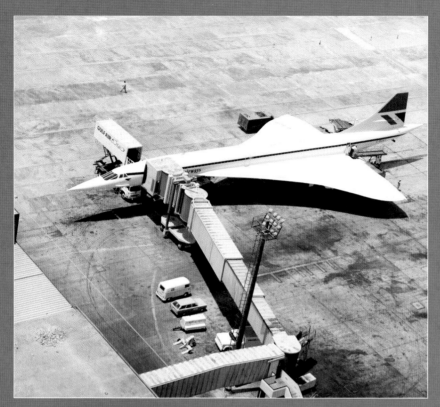

Syria and down towards Bahrain. Some 280 miles from Bahrain the descent was started. Fuel now had to be transferred forward. Reverse thrust was selected on two engines in order to increase our rate of descent, allowing us to make a straight-in approach to Runway 12. We touched down in Bahrain having taken 3 hours 17 minutes from the start of the take-off run at Heathrow.

My original flight in a Constellation from London Airport North had landed at Rome, Beirut and Kuwait on the way to Bahrain, and had taken almost 12 hours 30 minutes flying time for the same journey. How things had changed!

We were greeted at the airport by an enthusiastic crowd of well-wishers and photographers, and were invited by the Ruler of Bahrain to a banquet at his palace. It was a superb meal and we had time to mingle with the other guests. After

the banquet we moved to the Gulf Hotel for another reception.

On the homeward flight the following day, with no restrictions after take-off, we should have been able to commence our acceleration almost immediately, but due to forecast adverse winds extra fuel had been loaded, most of which went into the rear trim tank. This meant that a subsonic cruise had to be flown in order to burn off fuel, making space for rearward transfer, which was something that had not been anticipated.

The rest of the flight to London was uneventful and less hectic than the outbound leg. On our return the whole crew was delighted to be invited to an evening reception given by Her Majesty's Government at Lancaster House.

I am proud to have been part of the team that had worked hard to make these first flights so successful.

not just at the proposed 7½%, but also at the basic 5%. This was bad news – it could have meant reduced TOWs.

Now, as an aid to power assessment during take-off, minimum levels of Fuel Flow and Jet Pipe Pressure (P7) were 'bugged' – a movable index set to the appropriate level on each indicator. Our partners at Bristol worked out higher bug settings that would be equivalent to 5% Contingency, but still within the capabilities of the engine. Thus the day was saved, we continued with high bug settings until the problem was solved. In the end the solution seemed so simple, it was the getting there that was the hard part – the reheat flame holder (gutter) sprouted five fingers and together with a reprogrammed Engine Control Unit created stability right up to 7.8%. Modification kits were delivered in 1978.

ABOVE Air France and British Airways Concordes made a simultaneous arrival at John F. Kennedy Airport on 22 November 1977 after the first supersonic commercial service to New York. *British Airways*

amount of over-boost one could take out of the remaining engines when continuing a take-off following an engine failure after V1 – basically another 30C° of Turbine Entry Temperature and a bit more reheat. It allows for higher Take-Off Weight (TOW) when otherwise it may have been restricted by temperature (of the day) or altitude. During 'hot and high' trials it came as some disappointment to find that reheat was unstable

'By appointment'

In November 1977 we picked up our first royal charter, to return Her Majesty the Queen and party of fifty-four from Barbados to home at the end of the Silver Jubilee Caribbean Tour. It was the first time that sector had been flown by Concorde. Performance specialists had

BELOW The raw power of four reheated Olympus engines and the sophistication of delta wing vortex lift. *Air France*

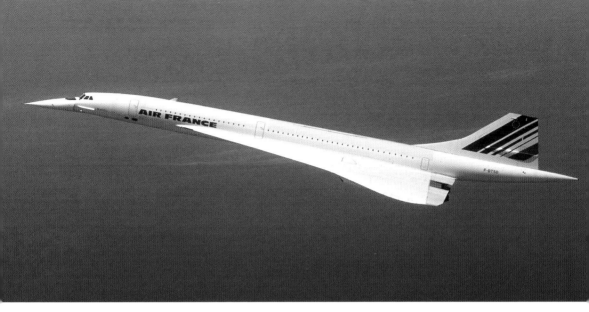

calculated that if new gutters could be supplied in time and high bug settings were used, then a TOW could be planned as though we had 6.3% Contingency, thus absolutely guaranteeing a non-stop flight.

As well as a quite splendid occasion, 'by appointment' so early in Concorde's life was a fillip to pride and confidence – not that the project was ever short of either. The aircraft, G-BOAE, was flown out, empty, two days beforehand. By arrangement, Concorde descended to 1,500ft over the ocean, spotted the Royal Yacht *Britannia* and her escort HMS *Antrim*, then dropped to low circuit height for a close-quarters rendezvous.

More intake work began in 1977. A stiffer rear ramp with a rounded leading edge, rather than a sharp one, was designed to alleviate a stagnation point vibration at around Mach 1.6. Fitment was held over in order to clear it with the 'thin lip intake' modification; this latter point, a piece of real magic. From in-service analysis Bristol had noticed that in the quest to provide good mass flow across the relatively warm North Atlantic, intake ramps were running at their upper limit, compromising efficiency. Once again there was an elegant simplicity, if not in the maths then in the engineering. The intake lower lip was cut back by about 1 inch and thinned to 7½°, resulting in an increase of capture area, making more mass flow available and allowing ramps to take up their best position; fuel burn was reduced by 1,500kgs, surge margin improved

and CAA test pilot Gordon Corps moved to enthuse, 'we are able to fly the aircraft at Mach 2 right down to zero-g and up to sideslip angles of 2½° each way – which when you think of the speed you're flying at, are enormous changes in the flight path – and the engine sits there and runs perfectly happily. You can slam the throttles from one end of the quadrant to the other; you can do just what you like. We've done it all, all combinations of these things, and it just swallows the whole lot and goes on working. That in itself I think is the greatest single achievement on the aircraft.' And that from the man who represented the authorities!

A steady stream of improvements flowed from the manufacturers over these years. A revised refuelling procedure enabled up to 1,200kgs of additional fuel to be loaded. Landing at up to 130,000kgs instead of the normal maximum of 111,130kgs was authorised, giving both tactical benefit and fuel saving.

A higher speed decelerating approach was introduced reducing flight-time and noise as well as fuel burn.

An extended fin leading edge, and tapered trailing edges to elevons and rudders, all contributed to drag reduction. A further aft CG for take-off made it easier to juggle maximum payload and maximum fuel – and since the trimmed condition after take-off meant more down-elevon, which acted like flap, an extra ton of Regulated TOW could be bought. Cool!

ABOVE Visor down and nose to 5°, Air France F-BTSD prepares to land. F-BTSD is a special aircraft because she holds world records for the fastest flights around the world in both directions. She made her last flight from New York in May 2003. *Air France*

British Airways and Concorde

Much has been written and spoken about 'ownership of Concorde', a topic once popular among those parties with an 'agenda' and scant regard of fact. It is not a simple subject. Its roots lie deeper than one may imagine.

In the first half of the 1940s, Britain's and Europe's aircraft manufacturing were consumed by war, the continent ravaged and destitute. In the immediate aftermath, civil aircraft design leant heavily on wartime bombers: the Vickers Viking's origins lie in the Wellington twin-engine bomber, Avro converted the Lancaster bomber to the 10-seat Lancastrian, then produced the York and Tudor as derivatives. It was all that could be afforded.

But in the USA, Lockheed had produced the L-049 Constellation and Douglas the DC-4, built as military transports until 1946. Larger Connies and the DC-6 followed.

To re-establish Britain's civil air transport industry, government, manufacturers and the two principal airlines, British European Airways (BEA) and British Overseas Airways Corporation (BOAC) worked together. It was part of BOAC's brief to 'buy British' and to showcase aircraft to export markets. Such co-operation carried forward into the 1960s. In due course BOAC, Air France and 14 other operators all took out 'options to purchase' varying numbers of Concorde aircraft. By July 1972 BOAC were in a position to place a firm

order for 5, having arrived at a compromise agreement with the government over their twin obligations – to maintain a profitable operation and to showcase UK products. Remember that the complete Concorde budget in UK and in France was funded by the two governments.

Pan Am was the first operator to cancel its options; one by one, all but Air France and BOAC withdrew.

The Boards of BEA and BOAC merged in September 1972 to form the British Airways Board, the full company merger taking place in April 1974. Thus it was British Airways who completed the purchase of BOAC's five aircraft over 1976–77 paying £22.5 million for each, including spares and equipment.

By 1979 it had been agreed that the development of supersonic air routes raised 'unquantifiable uncertainties outside of an airline's control' and so the Public Dividend Capital associated with the purchase of Concorde aircraft was written off. A further rationale that swayed the government was the presence of five unsold aircraft, homes for which were being actively pursued. A BOAC cancellation would not have sat well with that objective. The quid-pro-quo to the 1979 agreement was an 80/20 split of Concorde generated profit, 80% going to the government.

By 1980, after Braniff's brief flirtation with Concorde, but with still no sign of anyone stepping up to join the supersonic club, British Airways gained approval to buy one of the five unsold aircraft under the same arrangement as the first five: aircraft 216, G-BFKX, was modified from 191 to 102 standard and joined the fleet in June 1980, as G-N94AF, but changed quickly to G-BOAF.

The operating agreement, current during that period, was far from satisfactory. Its end was precipitated by the government's unilateral 'cessation of support costs' announcement. An essential part of the Anglo/French Agreement was the provision of technical and operational support to all Concorde operators. For any other aircraft such funding is provided by the manufacturer, offset by sales of aircraft and spares. Since the two governments owned the Concorde project, lock, stock and barrel, support was their contractual obligation.

This was an absolutely crucial moment in Concorde's post-entry into service history. No support funding = no Certificate of Airworthiness = no operation – as simple as that.

Initial dismay was short-lived. A recently constituted 'Concorde Commercial Team' within British Airways chaired a series of meetings with Rolls-Royce and BAe to explore the whole spectrum of cost of funding and cost of ownership. The three company meetings became 'four company negotiations' as the government joined the discussions.

By 1983 there was a new agreement. The three companies had settled on a level of funding adequate to provide support, sufficient to satisfy CAA and to be paid by British Airways, from Concorde profit.

Arising from the same negotiations, British Airways bought a seventh aircraft (214, G-BFKW, re-registered as G-BOAG), bought aircraft 202, G-BBDG, as a source of spares, and bought out the government's complete interests and responsibilities in the Concorde project.

Following this purchase British Airways owned the British half of the Anglo/French project in its entirety. Yet another unique facet of the Concorde story.

It could be said that Concorde was the businessman's express. Indeed, British Airways' schedule timings to the USA were fine-tuned to their needs. Concorde sold speed – 3¼ hours to New York. At Entry-Into-Service British Airways flew to Bahrain, but the breakthrough came on 24 May 1976 with approval for Washington flights. It took until 22 November 1977 before New York flights began. Loads were high and services were soon increased to twice-daily.

Singapore came on-line in December 1979 but scheduled services were withdrawn in 1980. Braniff International dabbled briefly in subsonic flights between Washington and Dallas in 1979. British Airways added Miami in March 1984 and, after a successful charter series, began weekend winter schedules to Barbados in 1987.

Concorde charter flights began in a small way in 1978, with the business expanding to a peak of over 40,000 charter passengers in

ABOVE Christmas day at the Arctic Circle: disembarkation at Rovaniemi, Finland. *David Macdonald*

1988. A hugely popular package combined two classic journeys – ocean crossings by Concorde and Cunard's *QE2*. The World Air Cruise became a regular part of Concorde's portfolio – 100 passengers, a Concorde, a crew and a three- to four-week itinerary to top destinations, best hotels and great activities.

For sheer diversity of destinations, charter organiser Goodwood Travel was the innovator. And the most memorable? Not what you may think. Without a doubt it was bringing the aeroplane to the people who paid for it – the British public. The Channel Supersonic, the North Sea Supersonic, 1 hour 40 minute flights, Mach 2, 55,000ft and champagne all the way. The flights were filled with all sorts of different people – family groups, anniversaries and surprise outings – everyone was guaranteed a flight deck visit and the cabin crew worked miracles. If one could bottle that spirit, what a world it would be!

BELOW A birthday present to the late Queen Mother – Concorde for a day, 1985. *David Macdonald*

The American adventure – type certification and Braniff preparation took the best part of two years superimposed onto an already busy programme. Quite bizarrely, Federal Express joined in with a request for a Concorde freighter. The study was completed, costed and found to be feasible, but fortunately the interest waned. Shortly afterwards, however, up to 1,500kgs of high value packages began to appear in the holds. Thanks Fedex!

On 2 June 1978 the first public sale charter flight was operated. Who would have thought that it would prompt such an explosion of interest, culminating in visits to 375 airfields worldwide? At the busiest period, in the late-1980s, charters provided 28% of total passenger numbers.

In June 1980 British Airways bought a sixth aircraft, G-BFKX, aircraft 216; built to the factory-standard model 191 Spec, she was converted to the BA's 102 version, re-registered as G-N94AF (the quick-change Anglo/USA registration), becoming G-BOAF upon termination of the Braniff contract. From 6 February 1980 onwards BA had leased aircraft 214, G-BFKW without conversion, finally

ABOVE G-N94AB at Bahrain, the Entry-into-Service destination.
David Macdonald

BELOW With fire streaming from her port wing, Air France's Concorde Flight AF4590 climbs away from Paris-Charles de Gaulle airport only to crash in flames seconds later. *Toshihiko Sato/PA Photos/EMP.2695971*

completing a purchase on 1 April 1984 after a partial standardisation. Prior to purchase, KW, or BOAG as she became, had been grounded for approximately three years. She had been the last aircraft due to be hangared for a major mandatory modifications lay-off but was still owned by the government, who were unwilling to pay the bill: there was no case for BA to pay for work on an aircraft that was still up for sale. Thus, not until an agreement to purchase was concluded between BA and the government was the aircraft taken into work. That was the reason for the three-year lay-off, not water in the hydraulics as had been widely reported,

The 12,000 hour Major Check became due on the first five aircraft over the years 1988–89. Twelve years of service history plus the findings from these examinations would form the basis of the 'Life Extension Dossier'. Minimum guaranteed life had been established, by the Farnborough Fatigue Test Specimen, at 6,700 cycles, that is 6,700 supersonic flights each beginning with a TOW greater than 170,000kgs. Flights at lower TOWs are factored down to less than one cycle and so the term Reference Flight (RF) was introduced.

On the 21st anniversary of EIS, life extension was confirmed by the Authorities at 8,500 RFs, without any work required. At last, pay-back time. That same high temperature that embrittled electrical insulation, hardened hydraulic seals, cracked fuel tank sealant and generally made a nuisance of itself was, all along, taking care of structure. Over 21 years there had been no corrosion. In the aviation world that is remarkable, but entirely comprehensible – liquids simply boiled away. The revised life was good up to 2004; pencilled-in was an increase to 10,000 RFs to take service time to 2010.

And then the hammer fell, again and again. The tragedy of Gonesse, World Trade Center Twin Towers, Iraq and the loss of a buoyant air travel market. The dice were loaded.

In April 2003 the two airlines announced withdrawal from service. We had known from the tens of thousands of people who had visited us on the flight deck that Concorde was loved, but the response from the Great British Public during those final months was quite overwhelming.

ABOVE Alpha Alpha follows the Macdonald clan motto, 'by sea and by land', to her new home at East Fortune near Edinburgh. *PRM Aviation*

BELOW A classic. Alpha Foxtrot wheels round the Clifton Suspension Bridge during the 'round-Bristol-tour' segment of the final Concorde flight, 26 November 2003. The aircraft is now on display at Filton airfield. *Airbus UK*

There were only four nations capable of planning a transonic penetration with big planes: they all gave it a go. Britain and France joined forces to fly for thirty-four years; the USSR produced a fine aircraft; but the nation one would have put money on to have led the way, seemed caught between hesitation and hubris.

It all started so well. Stimulated, perhaps, by developments in Europe both Lockheed and Boeing set up permanent SST departments in 1958. In that same year, newly formed National Aeronautics and Space Administration (NASA), as one of their first acts, established an in-house SST research facility – echoing UK's study group it was named SCAT (Supersonic Commercial Air Transport). It was a major undertaking. NASA Langley took the lead, producing twenty design proposals ranging across blended wing, delta wing and swing-wing. Centres at Ames and Lewis provided power-plant data, while Edwards contributed information derived from military and experimental flying.

On 5 June 1963 President John F. Kennedy announced the 'National SST Programme of America'. It began as a design competition – proposals and full-scale mock-ups to be submitted by January 1964. At this first round the field was reduced to just two serious contenders, the Boeing swing-wing 733 model – to become known as the 2707 and the Lockheed L2000 delta wing. A further contest was ordered. In all there were four submissions and appraisals until, in December 1966, a 240-man team of assessors finally gave the nod to the swing-wing Boeing 2707-100 and the GE engine. Lockheed had considered the swing-wing design, but rejected it on grounds of weight and complexity.

However, the consensus in the USA was to leapfrog, rather than compete with, Europe. While Concorde design settled on Mach 2 and about 130 passengers maximum, the

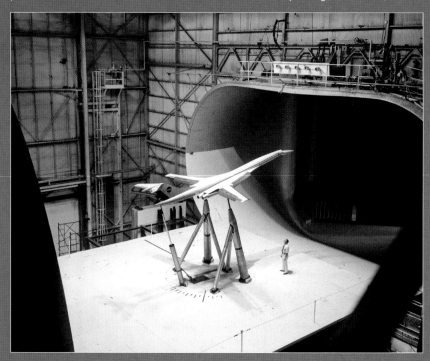

RIGHT Large-scale wind tunnel model of swing-wing Boeing **SST.** *Boeing*

American view aimed at 250–300 passengers and Mach 2.7 to 3.0 – an aircraft of up to 300ft in length and 675,000lbs take-off weight. (Concorde was 204ft and 408,000lbs.) The recently formed Federal Aviation Administration (FAA), whose early brief included direction to industry regarding new aircraft, were strongly of the opinion that high Mach numbers and swing-wing should be the American way forward.

It was a commitment to a stainless steel and titanium structure, to develop materials that would survive temperatures well in excess of those found in Concorde systems, to combat skin temperatures of 200°C to 250°C, to design an intake to manage an 1,800mph airflow and to produce a power plant to drive 675,000lbs of aircraft at Boeing 707 noise levels. Add a swing-wing mechanism, and that is 'hubris'.

They tried. A much revised 2707-200 was given retractable canards (version two of the Tu-144) to improve low speed characteristics; so much complexity, too much weight. By October 1968 Boeing dropped the swing-wing altogether, submitting a delta planform for appraisal in the following year – much to the chagrin of Lockheed. The 2707 in its -300 evolution became a double-delta, with a tail plane and therefore conventional elevators for pitch control, and a single-hinge, combined nose and visor.

But the knives were out. Ten years after the initial concepts, SST funding was still being channelled through the two government departments, NASA and FAA. Even the XB-70 had been seconded to the project between 1966 and 1968. It was beginning to make Congress unhappy. Ahead was the prospect of the agreed 75% government funding for manufacture, testing and certification of the aircraft.

On 24 March 1971 Congress voted to cease funding and on 20 May the project was formally cancelled.

By 20 May 1971 Concorde's flight-test envelope stretched from 126kts to 553kts and up to 57,700ft and Mach 2.075. Two aircraft were flying, having accumulated 113 hours of supersonic flight.

BELOW Full-scale wooden mock-up of the 2727-300 Boeing SST. *Boeing*

Chapter 2

Anatomy of Concorde

When the first glimmer of an idea was formed into a proposal for an SST, it was a giant-step moment, raising expectations from 300mph cruise to 1,300mph. Mach 2 was the natural choice; aerodynamic efficiency good, power-plant outstanding, environment challenging. Flight at the very edges of the atmosphere would be Concorde's home. A robust structure took care of in-flight forces, but temperature was the new dimension. Each material, system and component combined to produce an aircraft with the same high standards of comfort as any other – but she was, oh, so different.

OPPOSITE Aircraft 206, G-BOAA, under construction at Filton. Note the temporary undercarriage.

CONCORDE
6TH PRODUCTION
BOAC

General description

Fuselage

The Aérospatiale/BAC Concorde is a four-turbojet supersonic passenger transport aircraft. Concorde's fuselage comprises five major sections: nose, forward, intermediate, centre and rear, which are permanently joined to form a single unit. The basic structure consists of a skin supported by extruded stringers and fabricated hoop frames.

A single row of windows extends along each side of the pressurised cabin. Each cabin window comprises a pressure panel and an outer thermal insulation panel. Both panels consist of two layers of toughened glass separated by plastic interlayers.

The lower half of the fuselage is divided into various compartments to accommodate baggage, fuel, the nose and main landing gear and systems components etc. The upper half of the fuselage is occupied by the main cabin, the flight deck and a baggage hold incorporating a diplomatic mail locker.

The upper and lower halves are separated by a floor built as a number of sections and supported by a structure. The structure is free to expand longitudinally and thus minimise the thermal stresses arising from the temperature differentials between the fuselage skin and the longitudinal floor members.

The intermediate section of the fuselage houses the under-floor baggage compartment.

Wing

The wing is a multi-spar structure skinned with integral panels manufactured from pre-stretched planks. Easily removable panels, together with the general use of latticed and lightened internal members, provide access to any structure or fuel tank area even in the thinnest section of the wing. There are three elevons at the trailing edge of each wing.

Fin and rudder

The fin is a torsion box structure formed by a series of vertical spars and horizontal ribs which are covered with integrally machined skin panels. Attached to the torsion box are the dorsal fin and leading edge structure, the rudder jack attachments and their fairings, and the rudder hinges. The rudder is a single-spar light-alloy structure, manufactured in two parts (top and bottom) coupled together.

Nacelles

Each engine nacelle accommodates two engines and is divided into two structurally independent parts: the air intakes and the engine bays. An extension of the engine bays incorporates the secondary nozzles. The intakes and engine bays are attached to the wing by flexible joints which ensure complete sealing and continuity of form.

Who built what?

Franco/British Agreement
Article 1 (1) 29 November 1962

'The principle of this collaboration shall be the equal sharing between the two countries, on the basis of equal responsibility for the project as a whole, of the work, of the expenditure incurred by the two governments, and of the proceeds of sale.'

The engine companies had seen it coming. Bristol Siddeley Engines Ltd (BSEL) had signed a memorandum of understanding with SNECMA in November 1961. BSEL became

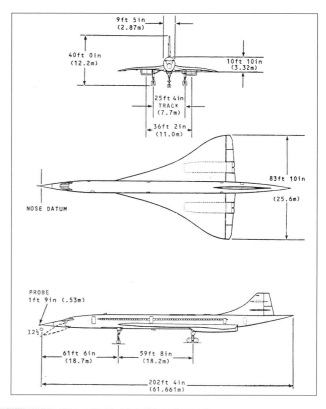

ABOVE Concorde dimensions.

LEFT French Concordes under construction at Toulouse. *PRM Aviation*

OPPOSITE The area-ruled ogival wing – 119kts to Mach 2.23. *John Dibbs*

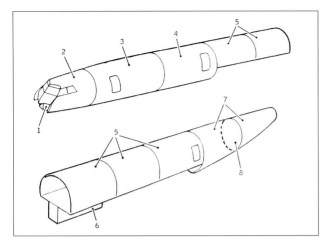

ABOVE

Fuselage Structure
1. Forward pressure bulkhead
2. Nose fuselage
3. Forward fuselage
4. Intermediate fuselage
5. Centre wing fuselage
6. Keel
7. Rear fuselage
8. Rear pressure bulkhead

part of Rolls-Royce in 1966. Translated literally, SNECMA (Société Nationale d'Etudes et Construction de Moteurs d'Aviation) becomes the 'National Company for the Study and Construction of Aircraft Engines'.

Theirs was a much easier accord. It was generally acknowledged that the Olympus was an engine of great potential. Thus in the event of an SST decision, BSEL would produce the flange-to-flange engine and SNECMA the bit behind – jet pipe, reheat, primary and secondary nozzles and some form of thrust reverser. On

the one hand, using all one's aerodynamic and metallurgical skills, develop the military TSR2 engine into a civil supercruise, every day unit, and on the other hand start with a jet pipe and turn it into something that produces 3 times as much thrust as its parent engine when at Mach 2. The job share was estimated at 60% BSEL and 40% SNECMA, hmmm?

Carving up the aircraft was much more complex. A glance at the breakdown drawing shows a certain logic, it also shows a construction logic; not a 204ft fuselage with a wing attached to either side, but a series of five transverse slices each comprising a piece of – left wing, fuselage and right wing. One doesn't need to be a stress man to see its inherent strength. So, France designed and built the wing, taking on the major task of creating an aerodynamic bridge from Mach 0.85 to Mach 2+, spanning the impasse of sound barrier and transonic zone. It was one of the most significant undertakings of the project.

Having the wing, it was entirely practical to take the flight controls, then their Power Control Units (power steering) and hydraulic supplies, the control medium from flight deck to PCUs and the electronics in between, viz. autopilot, stability enhancement systems (autostabs) and artificial feel; and so it was.

RIGHT 01, the first pre-production Concorde takes shape at Filton. The British Concorde prototype, 002, G-BSST, can be seen behind.

With UK having been awarded the engine, it was a sound decision to add intake and control system, on two counts – their interdependency and the fact that it was the other major fundamental.

With the big two allocated, it was a matter of practical division to accommodate a 60/40 split between France/UK. Fuselage, from nose gear forwards including nose and visor, and from wing trailing-edge aft including fin and rudder went to UK. France took the landing gear, however, since Dunlop had become worldwide industry leader in carbon fibre production they picked-up the brakes and, sensibly, the wheels as well; a nice set of light alloys – naturally!

Of the remaining systems, engine fire warning and protection, fuel, electrics and oxygen became British, while navigation systems, air data systems and radio were French. Then, presumably for reasons of balance, France gained pressurisation and air conditioning, but the UK took aircon distribution.

In 1962, each country looked upon the project as one of national prestige, and as one to consolidate its aviation industry on the world stage – partners by binding treaty, but as immiscible as the proverbial oil and water.

The structure

Fuselage

The industry classifies Concorde as a 'slender delta.' From the point of the standby pitot probe to the extended afterbody, the fuselage is 204ft in length, but only 9ft 5ins wide. To provide a context, the Boeing 777 is only 5ft longer, but at a whopping 61ft, is nearly 6½ times wider.

These are the numbers that aerodynamicists use to calculate 'fineness ratio' – the length compared to the width expressed as a ratio: for the 777 about 3.4:1. To choose an aircraft from Concorde's design era – let's say the Vickers Super VC10 – at 146ft long and 12ft 3ins wide we have a fineness ratio of 11.8:1. In the subsonic world there is only slight drag rise as girth increases, but on the other side – of the barrier – the rules change. Shock waves introduce wave drag, an element of which, zero

lift wave drag, is very sensitive to fineness ratio. Let's see where Concorde fits in. Prototypes at 184ft 6ins in length had a fineness ratio of 19.6:1. Pre-prod were increased in size for commercial reasons, range and payload; at 193ft, fineness ratio became 20.5:1. Production aircraft (and pre-prod 102) were given that extended afterbody – which actually made a good-looking aircraft even more handsome – specifically to increase fineness ratio, at 204ft in length it became 21.7:1.

With this decade's embrace of carbon fibre-style composites in mind Concorde's structure could be considered to have been entirely conventional were it not for the wing/fuselage/wing lateral slices and the omnipresent temperature. Design for pressurisation loads and 600mph was well understood, but to heat soak a structure at 130°C for 3 hours was absolutely new. Once again there was the two aircraft concept, one to fly full endurance in subsonic conditions and the other to complete a full range supersonic profile. One material, comfortable in a subsonic regime, but perfectly capable of adding thermal stress to conventional loads every day for thirty years, without complaint.

The fuselage is basically a pressurised semi-monocoque structure. Hoop frames at

BELOW Four production Concordes (G-BOAC, AD, AE and AB) pictured under construction at Filton for British Airways in 1975. *Airbus UK*

1 Pitot head
2 Radome
3 Nose drooped position (17.5° down)
4 Weather radar scanner
5 Radar equipment module
6 Radome withdrawal rails
7 Radar mounting bulkhead
8 Visor operating hydraulic jack
9 Pitot head, port and starboard
10 Visor retracting link
11 Retracting visor
12 Drooping nose operating dual screw jacks
13 Visor rails
14 Incidence vane
15 Front pressure bulkhead
16 Droop nose guide rails
17 Forward fuselage strake
18 Droop nose hinge point
19 Rudder pedals
20 Captain's seat, First Officer to starboard
21 Instrument panel, analogue
22 Internal windscreen panels
23 Overhead systems switch panel
24 Flight Engineer's station
25 Swivelling seat
26 Direct vision opening side window panel
27 Observer's seat
28 Circuit breaker panels
29 Avionics equipment racks, port and starboard
30 Starboard service door/emergency exit
31 Forward galley units, port and starboard

32 Main entry door
33 Air exhaust vents, equipment cooling
34 Life raft stowage
35 Forward toilet compartment
36 Wardrobes, port and starboard
37 VHF antenna
38 Four-abreast passenger seating
39 Cabin window panels
40 Nose undercarriage wheel bay
41 Floor support structure above nosewheel bay
42 Nosewheel leg strut
43 Twin nosewheels, forward retracting
44 Spray suppressor
45 Nosewheel steering jacks
46 Telescopic rear strut
47 Nosewheel leg pivot mounting
48 Hydraulic retraction jack (2)
49 Retractable landing/taxying light
50 Ventral baggage door
51 Underfloor baggage hold
52 Forward passenger cabin, 40-seats in British Airways 100-passenger layout
53 Overhead light hand baggage rack
54 Cabin air duct
55 Passenger service units
56 Toilet compartments, port and starboard
57 Mid-cabin doors, port and starboard
58 Cabin attendant's folding seat
59 Stowage lockers, port and starboard
60 Fuselage skin panelling
61 Rear 60-seat passenger cabin
62 Cabin floor panels with continuous seat rails
63 Fuselage fuel tank roof panels
64 Conditioned air delivery ducting to forward cabin and cockpit

65 Fuselage conventional frame and stringer structure
66 Wing spar attachment double main frames
67 Starboard main undercarriage stowed position
68 Undercarriage bay central keel structure
69 Port main undercarriage wheel bay
70 Pressure floor above wheel bay
71 Rear cabin conditioned air delivery ducting
72 Cabin wall insulation
73 Cabin floor carried on links above stressed tank roof
74 Foot level cabin ventilating air duct
75 Cabin wall trim panelling
76 Dual ADF antenna fairings
77 Starboard main undercarriage pivot mounting
78 Inboard wing skin with tank access panels
79 Leading edge ventral Spraymat de-icing
80 Starboard wing main integral fuel tanks
81 Outer wing panel joint
82 Fuel/hydraulic fluid/air heat exchanger
83 Fuel/air heat exchanger
84 Engine fire suppression bottles
85 Starboard wing fuel feed tank
86 Fuel-cooled engine bleed air heat exchangers
87 Conditioning system cold air units
88 Engine bay heat shield
89 Outer wing panel integral fuel tank

90 Tank skin with access panels
91 Fuel pump in ventral fairing
92 Elevon hydraulic actuators in ventral fairings, fly-by-wire control system, electrically signalled
93 Mechanical trim and control back-up linkage
94 Dual outboard elevons
95 Starboard engine primary exhaust nozzle shroud
96 Combined secondary nozzles and reverser buckets
97 Starboard inboard elevon
98 Rear service door/emergency exit, port and starboard
99 Cabin rear bulkhead with stowage lockers
100 Rear galley unit
101 Rear avionics equipment bays, port and starboard
102 Oxygen bottles
103 HF notch antennae
104 Fin leading edge structure
105 Multi-spar and light horizontal rib fin structure
106 Lower rudder hydraulic actuator
107 Upper rudder hydraulic actuator in starboard fairing
108 VOR antenna
109 Upper rudder segment
110 Rudder aluminium honeycomb core structure

111 Lower rudder segment
112 Extended tailcone fairing
113 Tail navigation light
114 Fuel jettison
115 Flight data recorder
116 Nitrogen bottle
117 Retractable tail bumper
118 Fin rear spar and tail bumper support bulkhead
119 Fin spar attachment joints
120 Rear fuel transfer tank
121 Fin spar support structure
122 Rear pressure bulkhead
123 Starboard side baggage door
124 Rear baggage compartment
125 Wing trailing edge root fairing
126 Port inboard elevon
127 Machined elevon hinge rib
128 Inboard elevon actuator in ventral fairing
129 Port wing rear main and feed integral fuel tanks
130 Machined wing spars
131 Inter-spar lattice rib structure
132 Combined tank end wall/nacelle mounting rib
133 Main engine mountings

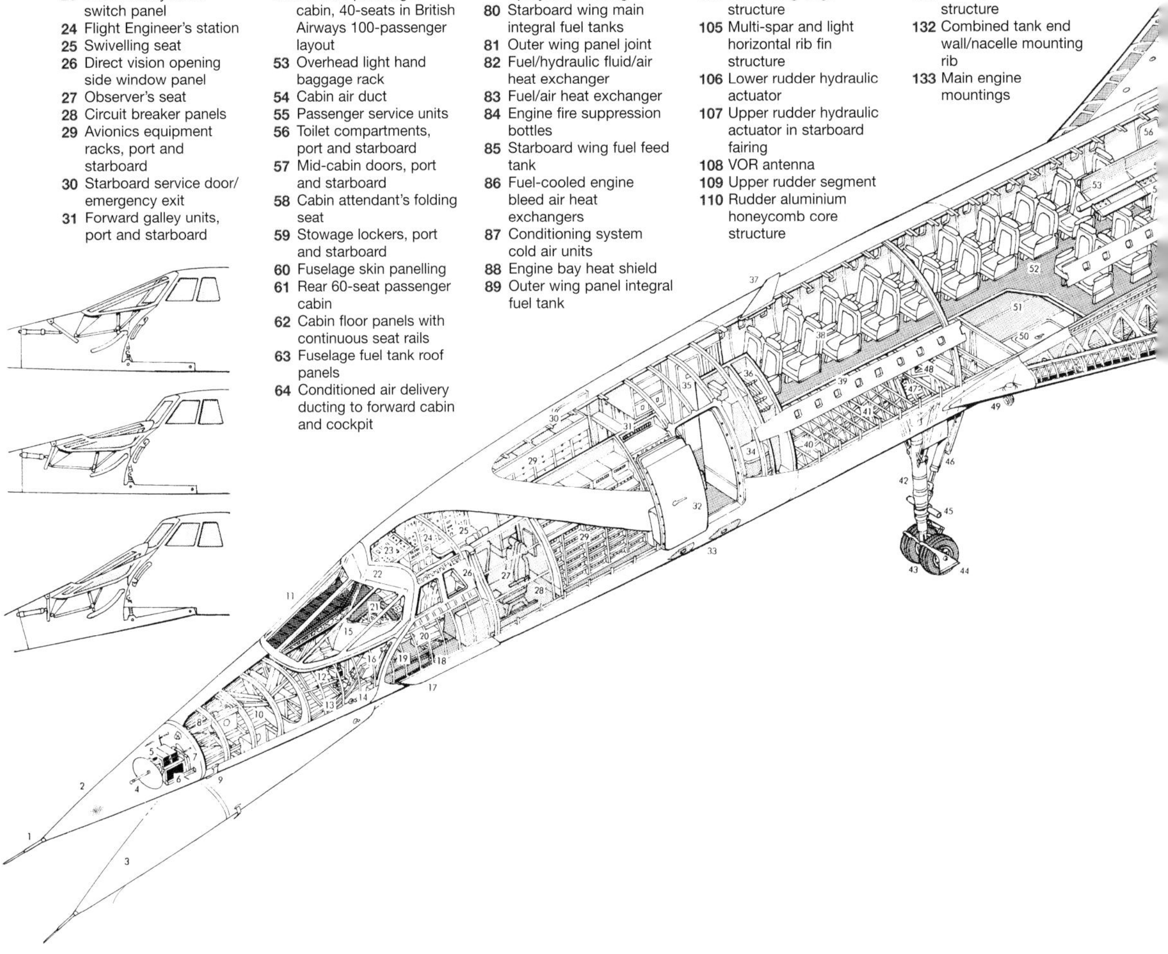

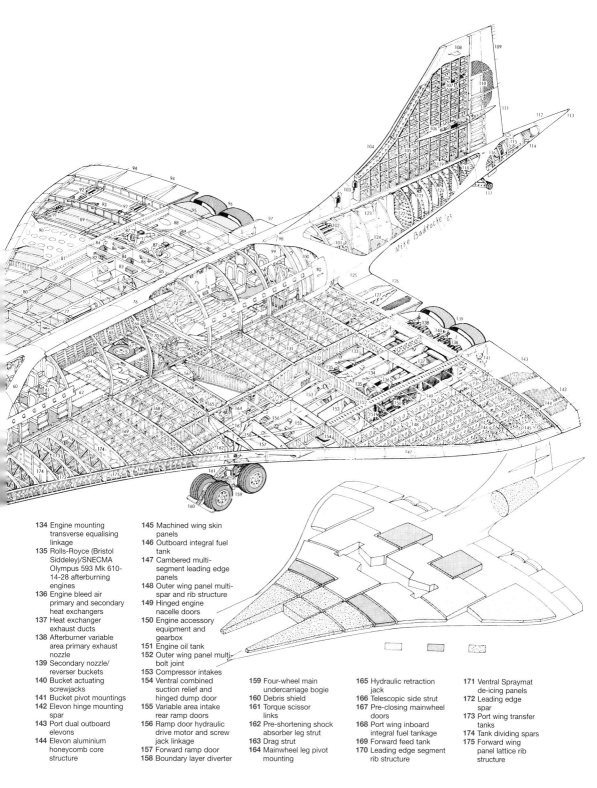

134 Engine mounting transverse equalising linkage
135 Rolls-Royce (Bristol Siddeley)/SNECMA Olympus 593 Mk 610-14-28 afterburning engines
136 Engine bleed air primary and secondary heat exchangers
137 Heat exchanger exhaust ducts
138 Afterburner variable area primary exhaust nozzle
139 Secondary nozzle/ reverser buckets
140 Bucket actuating screwjacks
141 Bucket pivot mountings
142 Elevon hinge mounting spar
143 Port dual outboard elevons
144 Elevon aluminium honeycomb core structure

145 Machined wing skin panels
146 Outboard integral fuel tank
147 Cambered multi-segment leading edge panels
148 Outer wing panel multi-spar and rib structure
149 Hinged engine nacelle doors
150 Engine accessory equipment and gearbox
151 Engine oil tank
152 Outer wing panel multi-bolt joint
153 Compressor intakes
154 Ventral combined suction relief and hinged dump door
155 Variable area intake rear ramp doors
156 Ramp door hydraulic drive motor and screw jack linkage
157 Forward ramp door
158 Boundary layer diverter

159 Four-wheel main undercarriage bogie
160 Debris shield
161 Torque scissor links
162 Pre-shortening shock absorber leg strut
163 Drag strut
164 Mainwheel leg pivot mounting

165 Hydraulic retraction jack
166 Telescopic side strut
167 Pre-closing mainwheel doors
168 Port wing inboard integral fuel tankage
169 Forward feed tank
170 Leading edge segment rib structure

171 Ventral Spraymat de-icing panels
172 Leading edge spar
173 Port wing transfer tanks
174 Tank dividing spars
175 Forward wing panel lattice rib structure

21½ inches pitch define the cross-section form and support both machined and rolled skin panels; the whole stiffened by longitudinal stringers. But it's not that simple. There is the division of responsibility and the manner in which the joint organisation fed from the two participating aircraft companies. The overall concept was agreed at, and published by, the very top of the technical chain. There are general arrangement drawings signed by both Lucien Servanty and Dr William Strang that show the form of the aircraft. Beyond that level each team had full design authority with the proviso that all drawings and proposals were shared with each other. Within the fuselage it led to a fundamentally different approach to structural integrity. TSS standards allow for 'fail safe' design, whereby any small crack will not develop to hazardous size before it is found by routine inspection; it also allows for 'safe life', ie the structure is safe for a guaranteed period. Both were perfectly satisfactory design standards and were approved by both certificating authorities.

The French fuselage, including those five lateral slices, built in unit with the wings, was designed to safe life principles, while the British portions, front and rear, were fail safe. A visible difference between the two philosophies became evident after paint stripping prior to the Major Check. From window line to window line across the top of the fuselage Bristol used three skin panels overlapping at 10 o'clock and 2 o'clock, while Toulouse used two, overlapping at 12 o'clock.

In the Concorde world much has been said and written about the 'Crown Area', basically the roof area between centre doors and rear doors. In 1980 a service aircraft was wired-up with strain gauges and a recorder. It showed peak stress in the crown area during take-off to be a little higher than predicted; as the rear of the aircraft squats during rotation and the total mass of front cabin, hold, galley, electronics racks and flight deck is heaved off the runway, the whole crown area is put into tension. It was nothing of immediate concern, but in due course a deep inspection programme was devised, to be added to the 12,000-hour Major Check becoming due in 1988.

The Major Check was a tricky affair. It involved unzipping the major production joints between the first four lateral slices plus the connection to the forward fuselage, each one from window line, across the roof, to window line. Ideally, the aircraft would have been jigged, as in production, but it just wasn't possible. However, Aerospatiale devised a system of jacking and trestling whereby a particular load was carried at each support point; each load being continuously monitored and adjusted as required. Frames 41, 46, 54, 60 and 66 were examined.

At Frames 41, 54 and 60 – one row of rivets each side of the join were drilled-out purely to crack-check the holes using an eddy-current technique, while inside, the last rivet at each end of the fishplates that connected the stringer ends across the join were similarly removed for inspection.

At Frame 66 – just the stringer ends were inspected.

At Frame 46 – two rows of rivets were removed from each side of the join, plus internal stringer ends. It was at this join that an external butt-strap was fitted to assist in the support of take-off tensile loads.

Closing each zip made use of an interesting cold-work technique developed by the Boeing Aeroplane Company. On completion of inspections, each hole was drilled and reamed oversize. The holes were further expanded using a pneumatic pump and a profiled interference-fit mandrel. Following a second NDT check, the holes were closed using special bull-nose interference-fit fasteners. The nett

BELOW Doors
1. Forward passenger/crew
2. Intermediate passenger/crew
3. Rear cabin service
4. Rear galley drain
5. Oxygen charging (passenger)
6. Oxygen charging (crew)
7. Upper baggage compartment
8. Rear cabin service
9. Intermediate cabin service
10. Forward cabin service
11. Forward toilet service compartment
12. Electrical ground power
13. Water charging compartment

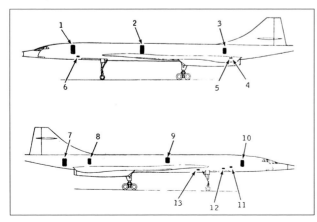

1 Cabin interior stripped for major maintenance. *Jonathan Falconer*

2 Forward starboard toilet, 2001. *PRM Aviation*

3 Overhead passenger amenity unit. *Jonathan Falconer*

4 Cabin crew intercom call panel. *Jonathan Falconer*

5 Seat belt, final version. *Jonathan Falconer*

6 The latest light-weight leather seats, fitted to BA's Concorde fleet in 2001. *PRM Aviation*

7 Overhead luggage bin, 2001. *Jonathan Falconer*

8 Rear cabin service door and passenger emergency exit, starboard side. Stirrup handle on right locks/unlocks door; upper left red lever is just a grab-handle; small dull-red lever between other two is 'doors to manual/automatic' control. *Jonathan Falconer*

ABOVE **The Convair B-58 Hustler, showing a basic triangular delta wing.** *PRM Aviation*

The delta wing

The delta wing is a triangle. The fourth letter of the Greek alphabet is 'delta;' its capital form is a triangle. Delta wings take on various forms, viz. basic triangle found on the B-58 Hustler, double delta where sweepback becomes less acute at some point as in the later Tu-144 and 'ogival' as on Concorde. Interesting that Tupolev began with an ogival planform but changed to double delta, whereas the ogive in BAC/Sud's hands was modified and refined to become a Mach 2 wing par-excellence. Let's see how.

At the drawing board and wind tunnel phase, it was found that several benefits would accrue if the apex of the delta was extended forwards: it introduced an element of area ruling thus reducing drag and also provided additional fuel tankage at a location that raised the prospect of trimming the aircraft by moving the Centre of Gravity in step with the Centre of Pressure, (fuel transfer).

A thin wing is a prerequisite for Mach 2 flight. In this context 'thinness' is the ratio between depth of wing and chord length. The delta, by definition, has a very long chord, thus an aerodynamically thin wing can still have good strength and fuel capacity. In Concorde's case 3% ratio at the root and 2.15% at the curved outer wing gives a quite exceptional reduction in supersonic wave drag while retaining stiffness and strength.

While the structure is stiff it is not rigid, there is some give, some elasticity. It was found that the prototypes' outer wing sections, under the influence of supercruise lifting force did not quite take-up the planned shape for best efficiency: the modular wing design enabled revised sections to be fitted. Similarly, aerodynamic interaction with intakes, causing engine surge, required new leading edges of a different profile.

In a wonderful example of design synergy, the same wing that is exactly right for Mach 2 also handles like a dream at take-off and landing, without any shape-changing flaps or slats. As Concorde begins a speed reduction in preparation for approach and landing, coming through about 270kts, a sensitive person may detect a bit of an aerodynamic burble. It is the beginning of a flow separation along the leading edges (every other 'plane is at pains to keep a smooth flow firmly attached to the wing). As speed reduces further, Concorde adopts an increasingly nose-up attitude and it is this change that encourages the separation to mature into two big rolling vortices, their resultant low pressure creating low speed lift. Reduction of speed, increase in angle-of-attack and vortex strength go hand in hand.

How remarkable to consider that a wing humming along at 22 miles/min, could, half an hour later be flown right down to just 2 miles/min. There is a downside; although the aircraft has demonstrated flight down to 119kts, there is so much drag in this area that even at full power the aircraft would descend at about 7,000ft/min right at the edge of controllability – but that is way outside the normal flight envelope!

In service flying, the minimum approach speed is 150kts and the maximum airspeed (not groundspeed) is 530kts, but what an achievement to demonstrate a wing that works from 119 right up to 573kts.

LEFT Elevons are attached to the wing trailing edge. *Jonathan Falconer*

BELOW Curve, camber and a thin, thin wing. *Jonathan Falconer*

BOTTOM Retractable landing lights are set into the wing apex, and the nose-gear door. *Jonathan Falconer*

result produced localised compressions that actually improved the zone's tolerance to the indigenous tensile loads. Because of its high cost, the technique was used strictly as a 'repair' process.

Statistics: Holes – 1508. Cracks – NIL.

Wings

The wing was designed and built in France. It seems unusual to describe it in the singular; other aircraft have 'straight wings' or 'swept-back wings', Concorde has a delta wing. It is obvious, really, one word to describe the shape formed by two wings. Now see the production plan, where two wings are formed by one shape: semantics and engineering in perfect concord.

The wing can be broken down into nine distinct sections plus a number of smaller parts – on paper. In reality five major sections were fixed for life during construction: these, the big five, are lateral slices comprising wing/fuselage/wing and together they form the structural heart of the aircraft. The highly-swept, forward extensions to the wing are attached to fuselage frames at three positions, and to the first of the lateral slices by a double ring of countersunk bolts. The fuel boys linked the pair together to form Tank 9, a forward trim (green) tank. Outer wing sections, too large and too curved to be termed wing tips, attach to main structure via 340 high tensile steel bolts: these also were

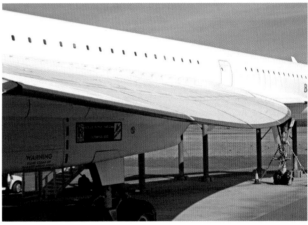

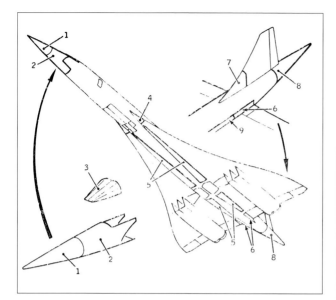

Fuselage Aerodynamic Fairings

1. Radome
2. Nose fairing
3. Visor
4. Leading edge fairing
5. Under wing fairing
6. Trailing edge fairing
7. Dorsal fin
8. Tail cone
9. Fuselage/wing fillet

booked for fuel, becoming Tanks 5A and 7A, and yes, they do link to 5 and 7 respectively. Note that fuel tanks were created from all wing space with the exception of zones immediately above the engines: these were designated 'dry bays' and contain valves, heat exchangers and other equipment plus engine fire extinguisher bottles. Finally, the leading edges, built in 4ft sections, they are bolted to a 'leading edge spar' formed at the outer edges of the main central structure.

Aluminium alloy RR.58, sometimes termed 'Hiduminium alloy', is used throughout. The long chord of a delta wing (leading edge to trailing edge) doesn't lend itself to classic main spar, secondary spar, ribs, construction. Rather, the complete assembly may be regarded as an immensely strong multi-spar torsion box. Each sub-assembly is built from span-wise machined spars and longitudinal ribs, some machined into a 'lattice-work' of quite delicate appearance, others utilising pin-jointed tubular bracing. The major wing spars occur at fuselage stations 41, 46, 54, 60, 66 and 72, these being the boundaries of the big five sections. Note that it was the fuselage elements of these production joints that were examined in minute detail during the Major Check.

Wing skins are milled from the solid, allowing integral stiffeners to be machined and providing

Kinetic heating

It is well known that a heated metal structure will expand. After a supersonic heat soak Concorde's overall length would increase by 8 inches – becoming 204ft 8in. The only visible evidence being that gap – the one between the aft end of the Flight Engineer's panel and the bulkhead; closed on the ground, but of a dimension comfortable enough for one's hand to slip into during supercruise. The first item to be lodged therein was a copy of the, 'Circuit Breaker List', an A5-sized volume, containing exactly what it said on the cover. During an early Bahrain flight and a crowded flight deck, the volume was slipped into the gap to keep it safe, yet handy. Deceleration, cooling and reversion to standard dimensions trapped it, securely. It wasn't recovered until the following day's acceleration, kinetic heating and expansion. The final item to be so placed was the flight engineer's hat, a sort of signing-off gesture. This can still be seen inside G-BOAF, on display at Filton, Bristol, placed there by Warren Hazelby during the last ever Concorde flight on 26 November 2003.

In a more technical vein, an element of telescopicity was applied to the cabin floor, though nowhere was that evident either by visible gap or movement. Below floor level lengthy hydraulic pipe runs were fitted with telescopic expansion joints while electrical cable looms had built-in slack.

Temperature was a particular bugbear to the maintenance team. Replacement of hydraulic component seals was a regular task until use of a different material was approved; one that sacrificed low temperature resilience in favour of better high temperature qualities. Fuel tank sealant, even the very best available, would harden with temperature, then under the influence of an expanding and contracting structure, begin to display small cracks. But, as a problem, it was as nothing when compared to the Mach 3 Lockheed SR71 Blackbird.

Designers will speak of the 'heat equation' – heat in versus heat out. To manage the heat is paramount. 'heat in' is the sum of kinetic and solar heating; simply put, the cost of travelling quickly plus sunshine. At Mach 2, solar heating would still be a significant proportion of total heat, thus a predominantly white livery was essential in order to reflect as much of that effect as possible. Any change of livery had to be factory approved in order to retain a good standard of reflectivity.

This may raise the question, 'why is the SR71 painted black?' By Mach 3.2, its skin temperature would be of the order 320°C to 350°C. In comparison to Mach 2, solar heating is of much less significance. It now becomes much more important to radiate-out kinetic heat, thus the aircraft was painted with a special 'high emissivity' black coating.

As an aside, there was much conjecture during 1979–80 over Braniff's likely choice of livery had they continued; this was their gaudy, multi-hued 'Flying Colours' period.

'Heat out' is managed in two ways: fuel is used to cool engine oil, generator drive oil, hydraulic oil and contributes to cooling the aircon supply. The four aircon systems themselves supplied a continuous flow of

air at −10° C between skin and interior trim: the temperature increasing, as a result, to a comfortable room value before going on to cool all of the aircraft's electronics followed by overboard discharge at about +40°C.

ABOVE That hat in that gap! The flight engineer's panel inside G-BOAF on display at Filton. *PRM Aviation*

BELOW The Lockheed SR71 Blackbird has admitted to Mach 3.2. *PRM Aviation*

Specialist aero alloys

There have been two revolutions in the way 'planes are built since Orville and Wilbur first flew. Wood and fabric soon gave way to metal as better engines allowed for bigger aircraft. In the quest for lightness with strength, aluminium alloys have held an eighty-year hegemony. Carpenter to tin-basher and now, on to fabricator as composites take wing.

It is possible that Concorde will always look modern, probably futuristic. Strange to relate then, that those timeless lines were formed from a material patented by Rolls-Royce Aero Engines – in 1928! Working with High Duty Alloys Ltd (HDA) from the Slough Trading Estate, they devised a family of aluminium alloys for the developing aviation industry – and all with an RR prefix. HDA had built a reputation for carrying over clinical standards of laboratory work into volume production; they were granted exclusive licence for the manufacture of those metals. To pick but one example, pistons for the Rolls-Royce Merlin engine, of Spitfire and Lancaster fame, were made from RR.58.

Monitoring the mid-1950s SST debate, HDA picked from their inventory an alloy that combined not only the qualities required for aircraft production but one that retained its properties at high temperatures, especially in sheet form. Pre-empting the Anglo/French agreement to build, they were ready. Concorde is built from RR.58. As a material it has not been bettered.

Today when ultimate performance is required companies such as Ducati in their World Super Bikes and Cosworth in their Formula 1 engines use RR.58.

And what of HDA? Sadly they have succumbed to the blight that has afflicted much of British industry – MRSA – Merged, Renamed, Sold abroad, and Abandoned.

optimum strength through precise control of thickness and weight.

Main landing gear is located in the section bounded by spars 54 and 60. The engine is hung from spars 63 and 69, while spar 72 provides for elevon hinge attachment.

Undercarriage

'**G**ear check please,' calls the flight engineer, ever the gentleman, as he begins the landing checklist.

'Four greens,' reply his chums.

Four greens? Yes, one each for the main gears, one for the nose... and one for the tail gear.

Undercarriage is a fine term, by and large supplanted by the transatlantic 'landing gear', although with country of origin in mind, '*train d'atterrissage*' would be most appropriate. After all, the Flight Control Position Indicator has always been 'Icovol' – *Indicateur a Vol*! A search through the Concorde library does reveal a predilection for landing gear, so in the spirit of internationalism that is what it shall be.

Concorde's maximum permissible weight for the start of any ground manoeuvre is 186,880kgs and for the start of take-off 185,070kgs. At the point of rotation, the main gear, literally the centre of rotation, is loaded-up at 195kts as the rear end squats and the front end is hauled off the runway. Maximum landing weight is 111,130kgs, though in 1981 landing at up to 130,000kgs was authorised. Normal approach speed (Vref) varies with aircraft weight from 150kts to 162kts at maximum landing weight, however a Vref+7kts became standard in 1979. (*See 'Reduced Noise Approach'*.) At 130,000kgs, Vref was up to 175kts while on the day that something quite unpleasant happens and the aircraft has to make an immediate return landing, the maximum weight Vref is 207kts...238mph. These are just some of the figures that Messier-Hispano, the French landing gear manufacturers had to contend with.

The landing gear is a spring/damper unit providing suspension and damping by an oil/gas, ie, oleo/pneumatic medium. The oil is of the hydraulic system family, the familiar pink DTD 585, while the gas has been changed from

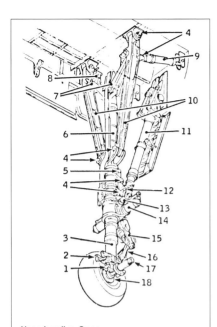

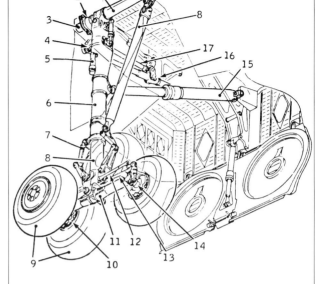

Nose Landing Gear

1.	Strut charging valves	10.	Brace struts
2.	Towing fitting	11.	Drag strut
3.	Shock absorber	12.	Up-lock roller
4.	Fork fittings	13.	Steering unit
5.	Interphone box	14.	Steering jack
6.	Leg	15.	Upper torque link
7.	Brace arms	16.	Lower torque link
8.	Brace link	17.	Wheel axle
9.	Actuating cylinder	18.	Brake

Main Landing Gear

1.	Cross beam	6.	Leg	14.	Axle
2.	Upper brace truss rod	7.	Torque links	15.	Telescopic brace strut
3.	Trunnion	8.	Shock absorber	16.	Actuating cylinder
4.	Lower brace truss rod	9.	Wheels	17.	Actuating rod
5.	Hydraulic sequence valve	10.	Brakes		
		11.	Bogie-beam		
		12.	Brake torque link		
		13.	Pitch damper		

LEFT Michelin Air X radial ply tyres, 2001.
Ian Black

RIGHT Main landing gear detail. Note the 'rooster-plume' spray deflector on the forward pair of wheels. *Ian Black*

FAR RIGHT Main gear cross-beam pivot tube, leg, side stay and drag strut. *Jonathan Falconer*

RIGHT Nose landing gear with 'bow-wave' flattening water deflector. *Ian Black*

FAR RIGHT Nose landing gear and drag strut. *Jonathan Falconer*

compressed air to nitrogen. First and foremost though the landing gear is a shock absorber; its job, to absorb and dissipate kinetic energy at landing; get that right and everything else follows on – usually.

But, during the latter phase of test flying as Concorde spread her wings abroad, runways with long shallow undulations were encountered. The combination of firm suspension, aircraft weight and a high speed encounter with just such an undulation at the wrong time was enough to provoke a continuous oscillation at the airframe's natural frequency. In the flight deck, cantilevered so far forward of the gear, the effect was of a lateral shake combined with a violent plunging motion of increasing amplitude. It was a wild ride.

It was found that for the take-off case the aircraft would benefit from softening of the air spring stiffness and easing the resistance to vertical movement in the oleo. Such modified main landing gear, the two-stage oleo, was introduced shortly after entry into service. However, a residual effect still remains. Taxying at heavy weight at Heathrow, the discontinuities between concrete sections would set the aircraft bouncing. Passengers would have been amused to see what looked like three gentlemen out for a trot. Once started, the only exit to the condition was to brake to a halt then begin again.

Gear location and dimensions, though critical are compromise. It is far from ideal to place the nose gear 40ft aft of the pilot; think turning at a taxiway, T-junction or following the centre line into an arrival gate between two other aircraft. Landing gear lengths are defined by keeping the rear of the aircraft clear of the runway at take-off and touchdown and then, in the case of the nose gear, stowage has to be found to cater for upwards and forwards retraction: rearwards retraction is out because of the need to plan for a free-fall mechanism.

In the main gear case, location was a real headache. At the only logical position, the legs would have collided as they retracted upwards and inwards, they were too long. So they were shortened – sort of. Whenever the gear was down and locked they were full length, but during the retraction process a mechanical linkage gradually and completely pulled up the

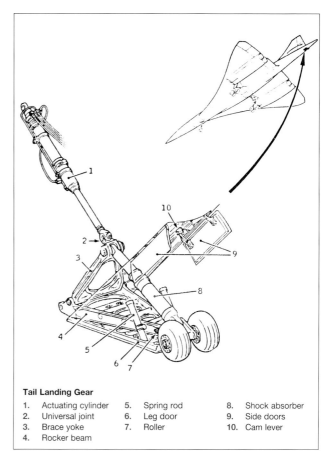

Tail Landing Gear

1.	Actuating cylinder	5.	Spring rod	8.	Shock absorber
2.	Universal joint	6.	Leg door	9.	Side doors
3.	Brace yoke	7.	Roller	10.	Cam lever
4.	Rocker beam				

BELOW Retractable tail gear and its oleo strut. *Jonathan Falconer*

hydraulics. It is accomplished hydro-mechanically and by manual sequencing and timing.

Certain combinations of problems would plan to preserve remaining hydraulic effort exclusively for flight controls. In these cases gear would be lowered by free-fall mechanisms. This involves a visit to the passenger cabin and much curiosity about the floor panels to be opened up, so it's best to fix one's confident smile in place.

Free-fall controls are located immediately above the nose-gear and main-gear up-locks. For the nose-gear a rotary control first isolates hydraulics and vents the retraction jack to atmosphere, then via a screw jack mechanism opens the doors up-lock and the gear up-lock (expect seven and a bit turns). The gear falls onto the doors pushing them open, the airstream catches the gear and pushes it into the down-lock.

Under the rear cabin floor a rotary control does a similar job on the main gear hydraulics, but this time a cranked lever is placed into a socket and, from a kneeling position with body braced and trying not to grimace it is heaved forcefully to starboard to open the up-locks.

In both cases a change in slipstream noise will indicate the measure of success. A practised hand will achieve '3 greens' within 2 minutes and 45 seconds. Don't forget to tidy up: then remind the pilots that the tail gear remains up!

oleo inside the barrel. A simple, effective and trouble-free solution.

A tail gear replaced the abradeable tail bumper. It is there to prevent the rear of the fuselage from striking the runway in the event of too high a nose-up attitude. Should the tail wheel touch on landing and its shock absorber compress, the first point of contact is actually the lower part of the secondary nozzles as they translate to the reverse thrust position.

Retraction and Extension

Retraction and normal extension is electrically signalled and hydraulically actuated. The gear up selection initiates a sequence of actions: if the up-locks are open and ready, the doors for the three principal gears are opened, then if nose wheel steering is centred and main bogies level, hydraulic pressure opens the down-locks, unlocks the shortening mechanism and retracts the gear. When up-locks are engaged, the doors will close. Extension is simpler: it checks that down-locks are open then sequences doors open, gear down and doors close. Tail gear basically follows the others, but is not involved in sequencing. Maximum speed for gear operation is 270kts; it takes about 12 seconds to retract.

In the event of hydraulic malfunction there is a standby lowering system using the standby

Brakes and Steering

Dunlop and Concorde changed the design of big aircraft brakes forever. Still powered from a main hydraulic system with an emergency operation supplied from standby hydraulics. Still a multi-disc unit using five rotors keyed to the wheel and six stators keyed to the axle, but now these discs are structural carbon fibre – solid discs of carbon fibre. Most of flight-test was conducted using conventional steel brakes, but all the while Dunlop was experimenting with carbon fibre and its production methods – then, more a black art than a science! In 1972 the first production unit was cleared for service trials on a BOAC VC10, to supplement lab work and rig tests. In 1974 they became the standard, for Concorde to fit and industry to follow.

Before considering the benefits of persevering with the new material it may be useful to recap precisely what an aircraft

brake must do. In Concorde's case, with the assistance of reverse thrust, it has to be able to bring 184 tonnes of aircraft from 165kts down to a standstill. In engineering speak it must convert the aircraft's Kinetic Energy (KE= $\frac{1}{2}$ mv^2) into heat and store that heat safely until it is dissipated either by natural cooling or by forced ventilation as with Concorde's brake fans. This is the classic rejected take-off at max weight from V1 (decision speed); steel brakes were alright, but at these high temperatures the discs displayed a propensity to weld together if the brakes were left on. The particular material chosen by Dunlop for Concorde's brakes remained stable at high temperatures – no welding or material degradation – had an excellent thermal capacity, a longer service life and the full set were 1,200lb lighter than steel. A win, win, win, win situation; congratulations Dunlop! To provide a context, after a normal braked landing one would see brake temperatures between 270°C and 320°C: as some of this heat radiated through to the tyres their pressures would rise from nominal 232lb/sq in to around 260. After a high speed rejected take-off expect temps in the vicinity of 650°C with some tyres beginning to deflate through their fusible plugs.

As with landing gear, brakes were electrically signalled and hydraulically operated. Within the

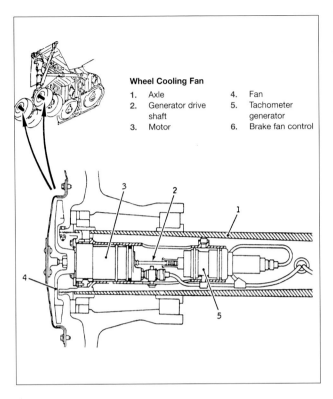

Wheel Cooling Fan

1. Axle
2. Generator drive shaft
3. Motor
4. Fan
5. Tachometer generator
6. Brake fan control

electronics was an anti-skid system, and torque control circuits to prevent over-torquing the discs at low speeds.

A brake control lever is located at the co-pilot's side of the centre console: fully forward for normal brakes, first position

rearwards selects emergency brakes – no electronics, but with an accumulator charged to 3,000lb/sq in; depress the lever's button and move to second rearward position for parking brake, operating via emergency system.

Nose wheel steering is entirely conventional: electrically signalled from either pilot's station and powered by main hydraulics with auto-change to standby hydraulics. Steering control handles will operate the wheels + or –60°; flight control rudder pedals will steer + or –10° while on the ground only.

Systems

How ironic to consider that Concorde, a triumph of Franco/British innovation, an aircraft that pushed the aerodynamic and propulsion boundaries to beyond twice the speed of sound, was the final classic airliner to be produced; an airman's aircraft, a thinking man's aircraft. Designed to be operated by three knowledgeable and fully participating airmen. A delight to fly.

It looks quite different on the outside because of the job it does; equally different inside because of the way it does it. All instrumentation is permanent display, showing all of the information all of the time. Everyone always knew what was going on all of the time.

Some of the aircraft systems have been picked out for special attention, the remainder are discussed in this chapter.

Air Conditioning and Pressurisation

In order to generate sufficient mass flow through the aircraft to help balance the heat equation, to cool electronics and to maintain a comfortable temperature, an air supply is tapped from each engine's HP compressor via a combined shut-off valve and 65psi reducing valve (bleed valve). Further downstream, the conditioning valve admits bleed air into the cooling system and thence the cabin: it takes 30 seconds to open to provide for a smooth entry of air to the cabin – no pressure effect on one's ears. Between the conditioning valve and the cabin, air passes through a ram-air heat exchanger, the compressor of a Cold Air Unit (CAU), a second air-to-air exchanger, a fuel-cooled heat exchanger, water extractor and finally is expanded through the CAU turbine. As an indication of performance, air comes off the engine at up to 550°C, the three heat exchangers take it down to approximately 90°C and the CAU extracts sufficient energy to lower the temperature to −10°C.

There are two separate electro-pneumatic cabin pressure control systems, each with a forward and rear discharge valve and cabin altitude selector. On a standard flight, cabin altitude would be set to 6,000ft; maximum differential pressure is 10.7psi. System safeguards will prevent cabin altitude from exceeding 15,000ft in the event of a run-away discharge valve. System architecture ensures that cabin pressure is maintained at a safe level long enough to perform a rapid descent to 15,000ft flight altitude should a cabin window blow out. Such an event has never happened, nor would it in a further 27 years of flying: cabin windows have two panes, a form of double glazing, each one capable of supporting many times the pressurisation load.

Pressurisation control is a hands-on system, under the control of the flight engineer who sets the desired cabin altitude and adjusts the rate-of-change to within comfortable limits. Instrumentation displays cabin altitude, differential pressure, rate-of-change and discharge valve position. It is a vital system – literally – and is attended to assiduously.

Note that during Certificate of Airworthiness renewal test flights (a 4-hour MoT), cabin air supplies are deliberately shut-down to perform the following tests:

- at 10,000ft cabin altitude an interrupted tone warning horn sounds
- at 14,000ft cabin altitude all the cabin oxygen masks deploy – the rubber jungle
- at 19,000ft cabin altitude verify correct oxygen pressure functioning.

The last test requires some patience; Concorde is a very tight aircraft.

On the 'ten to the minus nine' day when one is invited to scrabble beneath one's chair for a lifejacket, the flight engineer has a ditching

control to close-off all discharge valves to prevent ingress of water after 'alighting' at sea.

Electrics

At last, an area that may be considered conventional. Each engine, via its right-hand gearbox drives an Integrated Drive Generator (IDG), outputting 115 volts AC at 400 hertz (cycles per second) and rated at 54 kilowatts.

An IDG is a generator, a constant speed drive and a disconnect mechanism, all in one unit. The disconnect mechanism, solenoid operated, is controlled from the flight engineer's (FE) station and is used to stop rotation of the CSD and generator in the event of CSD oil low pressure or high temperature.

The CSD is exactly what is says; it allows the generator to be driven at a constant speed, therefore outputting a constant and accurate frequency, at all engine speeds. Its *modus operandi* is 'hydraulic' using its own discrete oil supply and a back-to-back hydraulic pump and motor assembly. A familiar fly weights-style governor controls pump output and therefore motor speed. Electrical load sharing circuits can bias the governor to maintain synchronisation when generators are paralleled.

A generator selector at 'ON' closes the Generator Circuit Breaker (GCB), a heavy duty relay, to connect each generator to its Main bus-bar. An identical unit, Bus Tie Breaker (BTB) will connect its own generator to a sync bus, thus allowing generators to be operated in parallel. Note that the Split System Breaker (SBS) has to be closed to connect left and right systems together. This is the normal mode of operation.

Each AC Main bus supplies its own AC Essential bus. Now, a bus-bar can be a metal strip or bar or arrangement of terminal blocks with a series of screwed terminals onto which individual circuits connect.

From the myriad of circuits in a complex aircraft, some are picked out as being vital to continued safe flight, while others are merely useful. Essential services, therefore, are grouped together on their own bus-bars so that when the chips are down, in the unlikely event of multiple failures, they can be powered from an emergency source; non-essentials can be shed. For this purpose there is an emergency (fifth) generator powered by a hydraulic motor and supplied from the Green hydraulic system. The fifth generator will power the four essential bus-bars, but not the Mains.

DC power is provided by four Transformer Rectifier Units (TRUs): system logic is similar to AC design. TRUs 1 and 4 are powered from AC essential 1 and 4 and therefore supply DC essential services; TRUs 2 and 3 are powered from 2 and 3 AC mains and are sheddable. Two 25 ampere/hour batteries connected to DC essential bus-bars via control switches complete the picture.

Caution

Aircraft 214, G-BOAG, built as a standard 191 model, was never fully converted to variant 102 specification. It still retains nickel-cadmium

Engine Bay Fire Extinguishing System

1.	Extinguisher bottle		(engine 2)	8.	Distribution pipe
2.	1st shot pipe	5.	1st shot pipe	9.	Spray nozzle
	(engine 2)		(engine 1)	10.	2nd shot pipe
3.	Directional flow	6.	Fire valve pipe		(engine 1)
	valve	7.	Pressure relief	11.	Delivery pipe
4.	2nd shot pipe		pipe		

batteries, and charge controllers to prevent overcharge run-away. Routine operation has the battery selector set to 'NORMAL', allowing the charge controller to connect battery to bus-bar, only when either is at a low voltage.

There are other smaller, specific purpose bus-bars, but the above description provides an overview of system design and function. One particular circuit will be drawn out as an example of electrical supply logic. It is well known that Concorde was the first civil aircraft to introduce 'fly-by-wire' electrical signalling to flight controls: obviously an essential service. This is how its integrity is protected: first there are duplicate channels, each with its own special inverter making 1800 hertz 26 volts AC (the rest of the AC system runs at 400hz, thus no possibility of harmonic interference) – these inverters are powered from DC essential – which in turn is supplied from AC essential – which can be connected to the fifth generator – which runs on Green hydraulics – which can be pressurised from the Emergency Lowering Ram Air Turbine (see ATA 29 Hydraulics), and this operates even with all four engines stopped!

Concorde doesn't have an Auxiliary Power Unit (APU), the tiny jet engine at the rear of most aircraft. (The APU starts from on-board batteries and supplies all electrical and pneumatic needs on the ground.) Pre-flight activity – crew checks, refuelling, etc – requires a Ground Power Unit (GPU), preferably rated at 90KVA or better. The ground power socket is on the starboard side, close to the nose gear bay; a lanyard will be needed to support the weight of the cable.

CSD oil is Esso ETO 2380. Built into the unit is an oil level sight glass with 'MAX/MIN' lines and an oil-charging point; a special hand-pump charging gun is required – there is no gravity top-up facility.

Fire Detection and Protection
Engine bay fire detection

Two electrically separate fire wire loops, co-sited in a perforated steel conduit, are located in nacelle doors and round the engine. In normal operation both loops are in circuit and both must detect a fire to signal a warning. If one loop is unserviceable, the good loop may be selected for single channel operation.

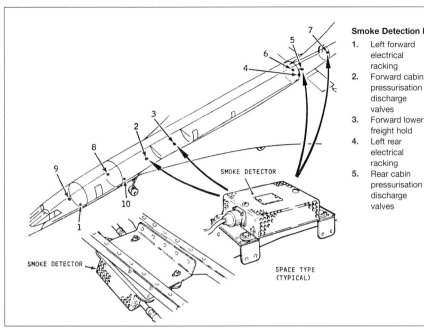

Smoke Detection Pressurised Areas

1. Left forward electrical racking
2. Forward cabin pressurisation discharge valves
3. Forward lower freight hold
4. Left rear electrical racking
5. Rear cabin pressurisation discharge valves
6. Right rear electrical racking
7. Upper rear freight hold
8. Right under floor electrical racking
9. Right forward electrical racking
10. Left under floor electrical racking

SMOKE DETECTOR

SMOKE DETECTOR

SPACE TYPE
(TYPICAL)

Ultra violet flame detection

Three dual circuit detector assemblies were strategically placed within the nacelle to detect flame break-out from any point of combustion chamber circumference. As their title suggests, they respond to UV light. Once again, both circuits must detect to signal a warning and, when necessary, single circuit operation may be selected.

(Note that this new type of detector was not reliable and was replaced by additional lengths of fire wire.)

Engine internal overheat

Thermal switches are located adjacent to bearings 2, 3, 4 and 5; any one will illuminate its 'ENGINE OVERHEAT' warning, prompting engine shut-down. Turbine cooling air temperature is sensed and presented on a gauge at the flight engineer's station; a 640°C thermal switch brings on the 'ENGINE OVERHEAT' warning.

Nacelle/wing overheat

This comprises a single fire wire loop in each nacelle adjacent to pressurisation bleed-air equipment and two thermal switches in a wing

equipment bay above the engine. Any one of the three elements, sensing a hot air leak, will trigger a 'NACELLE/WING OVERHEAT' warning.

Engine fire protection

One fire extinguisher bottle is located in a wing equipment bay above each engine. Each bottle has two firing heads and is capable of discharging into its own, or the adjacent, engine bay. In the event of an engine fire, first the engine is shut down, then the engine's own bottle discharged and if the fire still persists the adjacent bottle is used.

Fuselage smoke

Ten smoke detectors are strategically positioned within the fuselage adjacent to equipment zones and baggage holds. During Concorde's service life, toilet smoke detectors became mandatory and were fitted in 1987.

Fuel System and Centre of Gravity

The fuel system and centre of gravity (CG) are inseparable, they are as one; CG and flight controls are inseparable, they are as one. Highly integrated in function but not automated in control.

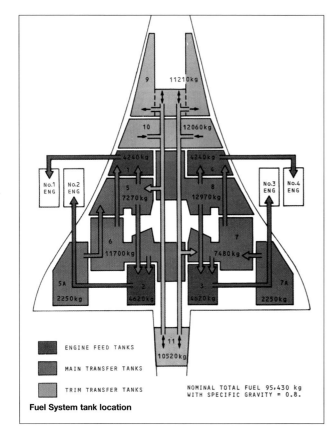

Fuel System tank location

9   11210kg

10   12060kg

4240kg   4240kg

1   4

| No.1 ENG | No.2 ENG | | | | | No.3 ENG | No.4 ENG |

5   7270kg   8   12970kg

6   11700kg   7   7480kg

5A   2250kg   2   4620kg   3   4620kg   7A   2250kg

11   10520kg

ENGINE FEED TANKS

MAIN TRANSFER TANKS

TRIM TRANSFER TANKS

NOMINAL TOTAL FUEL 95,430 kg WITH SPECIFIC GRAVITY = 0.8.

BELOW A typical fuel tank interior showing the fitment of Kevlar liners; upper and lower wing-skin machined construction; pin-jointed tubular and lattice-form wing ribs. *Air France*

If you look at any subsonic aircraft its fuel system is relatively easy to sketch: there will be one tank per engine, located in the wing adjacent to its engine, with perhaps an auxiliary tank outboard in each wing, a belly tank and maybe some form of tail tank for longer range. The whole layout is straightforward to assimilate.

Now look at Concorde's thirteen tanks set into the delta wing. Apart from using all space possible for tankage, its logic is not immediately apparent, but it is vital to understand form before considering function.

Only the Red tanks, 1, 2, 3, and 4 can feed the engines. The rest of the fuel is transferred into them, hence their alternative name, 'collector tanks'. Notice that 1 and 4 are ahead of the CG with 2 and 3 behind, so no change of CG as their contents vary.

Blue tanks, 5, 6, 7, and 8 are the Main Transfer Tanks. Their job is to keep the collectors topped up. Tanks 5 and 7 are an operating pair; 5 supplies 1 and 2, while 7 looks after 3 and 4. Once again they are disposed symmetrically about the CG so that no CG change occurs during their operation – note that 5 and 7 also accept Green fuel as part of Trim Transfer. When 5 and 7 are empty, 6 and 8 take their place and function similarly. The remaining 'Blues', Tanks 5A and 7A, are transferred into 5 and 7 upon reaching Mach 2.

Green tanks are Trim Transfer tanks. It is their task to shift CG aft by some 5ft during transonic acceleration, keeping it nicely matched to Centre of Pressure (CP). First, Tank 9 contents will be pumped aft to Tank 11. When that is full, the remainder of 9 will be shared between 5 and 7, where there will be room as they have been keeping the Red tanks topped up since before take-off. Tank 10 will empty into 5 and 7, whereupon the CG should be just about right for Mach 2. Study the fuel system controls (*see fig left and opposite*) to see how the Fuel Quantity Indicators (FQIs) and their pumps and valves are placed, then relate them to the tank locations.

It is stressed that none of the fuel is for trim purposes only, it is all usable and all multi-tasking, serving to cool engine oil, generator drive oil, hydraulic oil and aircon supply. It needs extra care, too. To prevent violent

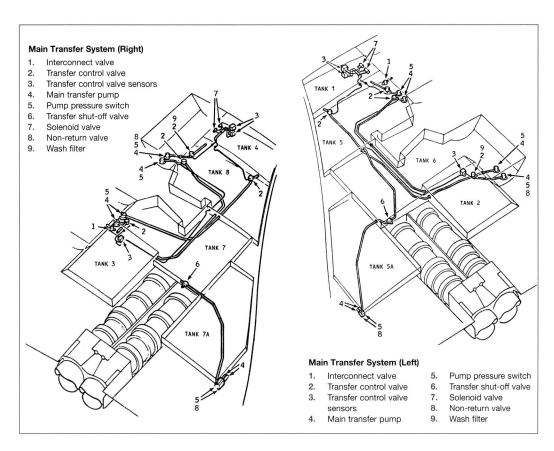

Main Transfer System (Right)

1. Interconnect valve
2. Transfer control valve
3. Transfer control valve sensors
4. Main transfer pump
5. Pump pressure switch
6. Transfer shut-off valve
7. Solenoid valve
8. Non-return valve
9. Wash filter

TANK 1

TANK 4

TANK 5

TANK 8

TANK 6

TANK 2

TANK 7

TANK 3

TANK 5A

TANK 7A

Main Transfer System (Left)

1. Interconnect valve	5.	Pump pressure switch
2. Transfer control valve	6.	Transfer shut-off valve
3. Transfer control valve sensors	7.	Solenoid valve
	8.	Non-return valve
4. Main transfer pump	9.	Wash filter

release of entrapped air during high rates of climb in thin air, the fuel in tanks not in use must be constantly agitated to provide gradual release – known as the de-air process (think of champagne bottle or diver's bends). Climbing through 42,000ft, vents are closed-off and tanks lightly pressurised to minimise evaporation losses in low pressure atmospheres.

And now to the CG and its travels. Correct CG placement is vital. Cruise speed cannot be attained with CG at take-off value – the aircraft cannot be landed (ie, it won't fly) with CG at supercruise position. It is as fundamental as flaps/slats to other aircraft – even more so, because a subsonic can always make a flapless landing.

As a general rule in aircraft design important things are duplicated, very important things are triplicated (there are three CG indicating systems) and critical things are quadruplicated – there are four pumps available in Tank 11

to guarantee forward movement of fuel, and therefore CG, to enable flight at approach and landing speeds, two pumps powered from electrical systems, one from left-hand hydraulic system and one from right-hand hydraulics.

But why go to all this trouble? Well, it is an elegant solution to an aerodynamic problem concerning Centre of Pressure (CP) and Centre of Gravity (CG).

CP is that point on a wing chord where the total sum of all lifting forces can be said to act.

FACT – as an aircraft travels faster so the CP moves further back towards the trailing edge of the wing.
FACT – The CG is a point where all of the weight of the aircraft can be said to act – a bit like a balance point.
FACT – an aircraft is loaded so that the CG is always ahead of the CP.

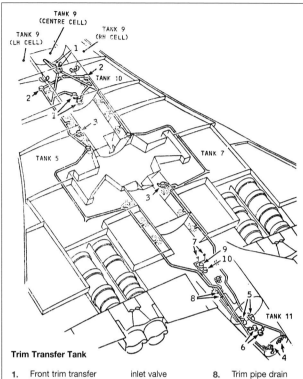

Trim Transfer Tank

1. Front trim transfer pump (electric)
2. Front trim tank inlet valve
3. Main transfer tank inlet valve
4. Rear trim tank
5. Rear trim transfer pump (hydraulic)
6. Rear trim transfer pump (electric)
7. Hydraulic selector valve
   inlet valve
8. Trim pipe drain valve (ref)
9. Hydraulic filter – green (ref)
10. Hydraulic filter – blue (ref)

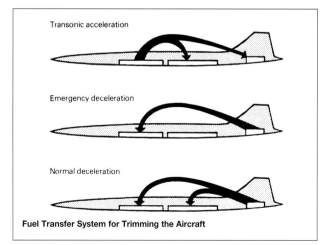

Fuel Transfer System for Trimming the Aircraft

As any aircraft increases its speed, and its CP moves aft, the tendency for the aircraft to tip nose-down would be corrected by a little 'up-elevator' or movement of the tail plane itself. Concorde, however, flies at tremendously high speed, thus its CP travels a whopping 5ft rearwards. To displace flight controls to counteract such a nose-down tipping moment would be hugely inefficient in terms of drag, so Concorde was designed without a balancing tail surface. As CP moves rearwards with increasing speed, the flight engineer pumps approximately 23 tonnes of fuel from those front Green tanks, first to make sure that the rear Green tank, under the tail, holding 10½ tonnes is full, and then into the wings, at all times keeping CP and CG matched and therefore the aircraft trimmed. After the front Green tanks are empty, small fuel adjustments will be made throughout supercruise to keep the six elevons all in line and exactly half a degree drooped – this being minimum drag for Mach 2 flight.

It is hoped that by now the reader has an appreciation of CG control and its significance to the safe and efficient conduct of supersonic flight. It is anticipated that by now the enquiring mind will have considered, 'surely there is some conventional form of pitch trim?' and, in terms of fuel trim, 'how is it known that one has got it right?'

First point – yes, there is an entirely conventional pitch trim wheel that adjusts all six elevons together, with a rocker switch on the control column to do the same job electrically (*see Flying Controls, page 63*).

Second point – just as a 'flight envelope' is published showing maximum and minimum speeds from sea level to maximum altitude, so there is an equivalent graph, 'the CG corridor', that plots CG against Mach number. The flight engineer will read it vertically; it will show him where CG must be at that instantaneous Mach number. Read horizontally it will show the pilot his maximum and minimum speed at that instantaneous CG. Cunningly, this exact information is displayed on instruments. The CG vertical strip display has the actual CG flanked by forward and aft limit bugs driven by a Mach number signal derived from an Air Data Computer, while Mach meters show actual Mach number with limit bugs driven by a CG signal. In general terms a CG too far forward would run up against elevon control limit, while too far aft (too close to CP) would compromise pitch stability. Thus fuel and CG and flight controls are inseparable – they are all as one.

Hydraulics

If the Electrics can be said to be the neural system of the aircraft, then Hydraulics constitute lifeblood and muscle. Without Chevron M2V coursing through the network of pumps, pipes and valves, the lights would be on, but nothing would stir.

There are three separate hydraulic systems – two main and one standby – colour coded and operating at 4,000psi. Green system is powered by a pump on each of engines 1 and 2, Blue from engines 3 and 4 and standby system, Yellow, from engines 2 and 4. All pumps are driven from the engines' right-hand gearboxes.

Since Concorde's flight controls are powered by the above, with no manual reversion, an Emergency Lowering Ram Air Turbine (ELRAT) is fitted into the port inner elevon fairing. It comprises a pivoting strut carrying two hydraulic pumps, one Green and one Yellow and a small-diameter, twin-bladed 'propeller' to spin-up in the airstream. The RAT pumps are smaller, the Green unit has a maximum output of 3,850psi and is primarily concerned with driving the fifth generator and powering Tank 11's Green transfer pump, while the Yellow unit looks after flight controls. When deployment is needed, the RAT mechanical up-lock is released by a duplicated cartridge arrangement, fired electrically from the flight engineer's station. It was never used in anger, only ever lowered on test. Occasionally there is reference to a 'HYRAT'. It's the same unit but with the prefix 'HY' to denote its hydraulic function.

To complete the pumping line-up, there are two electric Ground Hydraulic Check-Out pumps, only operable with ground power connected.

All three systems are similar in design. From the reservoir, a line to each pump passes through a fuel-cooled heat exchanger

and an isolate valve. Pumps themselves have a solenoid operated off-load control and a cooling case drain flow routed through a case drain filter back to return. It is vital to keep a close check on these filters; any restriction in flow can lead to raised case pressure and pump-case separation, with consequent system loss. Downstream, each pump output passes through an HP filter and non-return-valve before commoning-up with its partner to supply aircraft services. All return flows combine to pass through an LP filter before returning to reservoir.

Fluid must be supplied to pumps at a positive pressure. The Concorde method is to fashion the fluid container as a stainless steel bellows, then surround it with an airtight container, pressurised to 60psi using engine bleed air. A small electrically driven compressor is available to top-up the air pressure during ground servicing activities.

Reservoirs and charging points are located in the lower fuselage hydraulic equipment bay between frames 72 and 74 – remember that frame 72 is the elevon attachment point. A special hand-pump charging gun is required, there is no gravity fill facility, thus no opportunity to top-up in flight.

LEFT Emergency lowering ram air turbine.

1 Twin pitot probes, incidence vanes, temperature probes and moustaches, all in good condition; hatches closed. *David Macdonald*

2 Starboard pitot probe, seen here with its ground safety cover, supplies air pressure data to the co-pilot's instruments. *Jonathan Falconer*

3 Toilet drain panel, starboard static air pressure sensor plates and orifices. *David Macdonald*

4 VHF 2 comms antenna. The dart-shaped attachment is the ILS 1 & 2 glide-slope antennae. *Jonathan Falconer*

5 Rear galley drain horn; cabin pressurisation rear discharge valves outlets. *Jonathan Falconer*

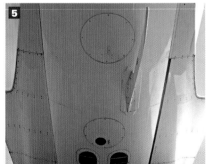

Navigation

Concorde has a navigation suite to cover all occasions from the macro to the micro. But navigation wasn't always so.

Electronics have revolutionised the art and skill of estimated positions and fixes into today's 60/60 certainty of Global Positioning Systems (Sat Nav). At the start of the authors' airline careers, Captain Dave Leney, then navigating Constellations, would derive an aircraft's position (a fix) from the following inventory: sextant and star shots, Loran – a US-developed version of Britain's wartime GEE radio navigation system, or even a fix from an Ocean Station Vessel. And, when all else failed, he would maintain a running plot of estimated positions based on 'dead-reckoning', a basic technique of speed and heading against time, taking into account the forecast wind.

Wind was always a quandary, whether head, tail or on the beam. In September 1989, during supercruise New York to London, a Concorde 004 picked up a distress message from a nearby small aircraft, some 50,000ft below. He was searching for the Azores, but it was apparent that he'd been blown hopelessly off course by an unusual, strong southerly wind.

By the simple rotation of the Inertial Navigation System (INS) data selector to the 'WIND' position Concorde could see 180°/20kts, a southerly wind at a speed of 20kts.

INS is probably the best aircraft navigation system ever produced, to date. It was born within the Apollo moon-shot programme and first came to civil aviation with the Boeing 747. Concorde has a triple system, one set for each crew member. It is an accurate, reliable, world-wide navigation system and is entirely self-contained: to be completely independent of ground station and satellite gave a high level of confidence.

At the heart of an INS unit are a triple gyro set and electronics that measure the smallest of accelerations. From acceleration is calculated speed and thence distance with time. Crew communicate with the system in terms of latitude and longitude and, in exchange, can select the following combinations of navigation data:

- current aircraft track (across the earth's surface) and ground speed.

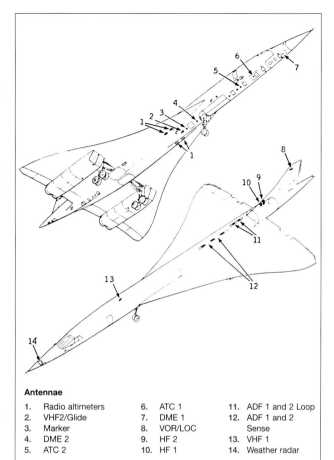

Antennae

1.	Radio altimeters	6.	ATC 1	11.	ADF 1 and 2 Loop
2.	VHF2/Glide	7.	DME 1	12.	ADF 1 and 2
3.	Marker	8.	VOR/LOC		Sense
4.	DME 2	9.	HF 2	13.	VHF 1
5.	ATC 2	10.	HF 1	14.	Weather radar

- true heading and drift angle (caused by any element of cross-wind).
- cross-track error (distance left or right from desired track) and track angle error (angular deviation between actual and desired track).
- present position in latitude and longitude.
- distance and time from present position to next waypoint.
- wind speed and direction.
- desired track between any two waypoints.

INS also interfaces with flight instruments, provides navigation guidance to autopilots and supplies gyro stabilising signals to the compass systems and the artificial horizons, in place of conventional azimuth and vertical gyros as used in the past.

During Concorde's life, much of overland airways and terminal area navigation was defined by radio navigation beacons; VOR (VHF omni-directional range) transmitting in the VHF band and ADF (automatic direction finding) in the medium frequency band. Both sets were operated in a broadly similar manner – the receiver would be tuned to a numerical frequency and the station verified by a two or three-letter Morse code identification. Interpretation was straight forward and instinctive, in each case a needle superimposed upon a compass card would 'point to' the station, thus informing the crew of the bearing to or from that location. Often a DME (Distance

Measuring Equipment) station would be co-sited with a VOR, the dual information of range and bearing providing an accurate position, or 'fix'. Concorde carried the standard package of two VORs, two DMEs and two ADFs.

At the micro end of the navigation spectrum comes the dual ILS (Instrument Landing System). Once the landing runway is known the ILS receivers are tuned, as for a VOR, to that runway's high precision Localiser and Glide Slope transmitters: these provide guidance onto and along the runway's extended centre line (localiser) and down the final descent path to touchdown (glide slope). When coupled to the autopilot such guidance is sufficiently

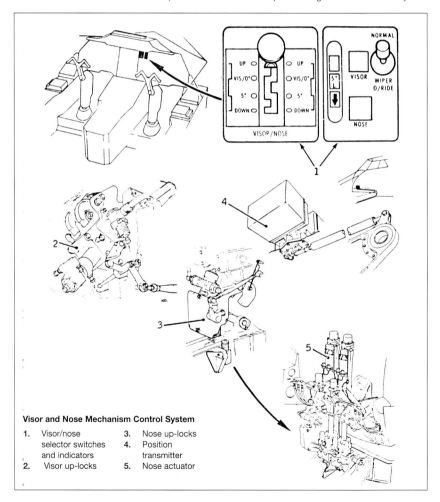

Visor and Nose Mechanism Control System

1.	Visor/nose selector switches and indicators	**3.**	Nose up-locks
		4.	Position transmitter
2.	Visor up-locks	**5.**	Nose actuator

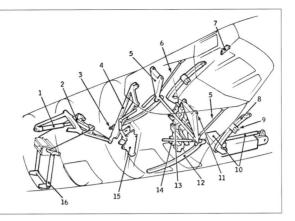

Visor and Nose Mechanism

1. Visor actuating jack
2. 'A' frame
3. Visor down micro switch
4. Operating leg
5. Tracking leg
6. Strut
7. Visor location fitting
8. Guide rail
9. Carriage
10. Nose transmitter unit
11. Side load links
12. Visor rail
13. Nose actuator
14. Nose up-lock
15. Visor up-lock
16. Spring assister mechanism

accurate, and of a proven reliability, to provide full automatic landing capability in reduced visibility conditions; Concorde's autoland visibility limits were 250 metres horizontally and 15ft decision height.

Nose and visor

If there is one view of Concorde that is an icon of its times, it must be the nose. Whether raised to display the full elegance of a supersonic shape, or lowered as part of the 'bird of prey' image at landing.

However one sees it, the *raison d'être* is simply to improve the pilots' forward and downward view of the runway at landing.

All the contenders had one: the Tu-144, a one-piece combination nose/visor, the swing-wing Boeing, showing its predilection for hinges, a double-articulated combination and the Lockheed, following Alexei's lead, a one-piece.

Thus Concorde is unique in having a separate visor that, at the first selection, slides forwards and downwards into a recess in the nose, then travels with the nose, first to 5° down for take-off and all flight below about 270kts, then to 12½°, fully down at landing. Each movement takes 5 to 6 seconds.

Both prototypes had a full metal visor with just two small glazed panels: from the pre-production 101, G-AXDN, onwards all aircraft were fitted with the fully glazed visor – altogether more attractive, both practically and aesthetically.

While it is normal practice to perform a take-off with the visor/nose at 'down and 5°', the aircraft can, and has, made take-offs with them both 'up', quite satisfactorily. However, should one consider an approach and landing with nose/visor up, then firstly, 25ft of nose would give a distinctly poor view of the runway and secondly, the wheels wouldn't come down! When the visor is raised, an interlock isolates the 'landing gear down' circuits – a positive preclusion to inadvertent gear deployment at Mach 2: for the sake of a few feet of wire, probably worthwhile. The interlock always released, it never interfered with a normal 'gear down' selection.

BELOW A nose and visor assembly is prepared for installation at Filton. Behind can be seen G-BOAB ready for delivery.

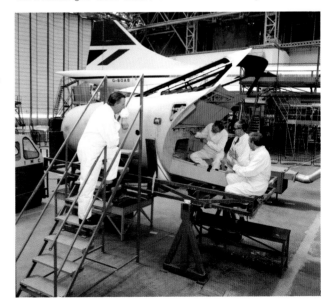

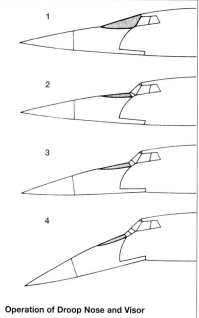

Operation of Droop Nose and Visor

1. Supersonic flight, visor up
2. Visor retracted
3. Take-off configuration
4. Maximum droop for landing

1 A paint-stripped G-BOAD with visor down and nose at maximum drop. *Jonathan Falconer*

2 Nose and visor up – a snug, streamlined fit. *Ian Black*

3 Flight deck sliding windows and escape ropes form the flight crew's emergency exits. Also visible in this picture are the left-hand pitot head, the incidence vane below the main windscreen and two temperature probes on the nose lower surface. Co-author Dave Leney is looking out of the flight deck window. *Jonathan Falconer*

4 Visor down, nose at 5°. The small strake below the cockpit side windows is one of a pair of 'moustaches' – their job is to stimulate a flow of air across the rudders at low speeds. *Ian Black*

The visor glazed panels are laminations of two plies plus a thin non-stressed interlayer; gold-film heating is applied to the inner surface of the outer panel. Total thickness is about ½ inch of heat-proof, very tough, impact-resistant glass.

When fully up, both visor and nose have their own mechanical up-locks. The nose 5° position is held by internal locks inside the actuating jacks. There are no down-locks.

Visor and nose are actuated by separate hydraulic jacks powered from the aircraft's Green hydraulic system, the selector lever being mounted on the co-pilot's instrument panel.

A standby lowering system, with selectors on the centre console, uses Yellow hydraulic pressure to lower the visor and to unlock the nose, allowing it to lower under aerodynamic force.

Just as with landing gear, the visor/nose can be lowered by free-fall, but only to the 5° position. A lever, on the starboard flank of the centre console, will open the nose up-lock mechanically, which in turn releases the visor up-lock – gravity and aerodynamic forces complete the movement.

Although flight up to 325kts and Mach 0.8

is authorised with visor down, anything above 270kts is very, very noisy. During flight-test, 350kts and Mach 0.8 had been achieved before visor was raised for the very first time on flight No. 11. Having become used to the 'visor down' noise level, the calm and quiet as it locked up, completing the aerodynamic shape, prompted worried glances at the engines to make sure that they were still running.

Initially 17½° was evaluated as the fully down position. It didn't find favour. Apparently there was a strong visual sensation of there being nothing ahead of one as the nose disappeared completely from view.

Flying controls

The aircraft is controlled in pitch and roll by elevons, and in yaw by rudders.

Control column movements are the same as for any other aircraft. There is no tail-plane and the elevons are placed along the trailing edge of the wing. The nose-up and nose-down movements are controlled by six elevons (mainly the inner pair). The middle and outer pairs also act as ailerons.

Concorde uses a 'fly-by-wire' system in

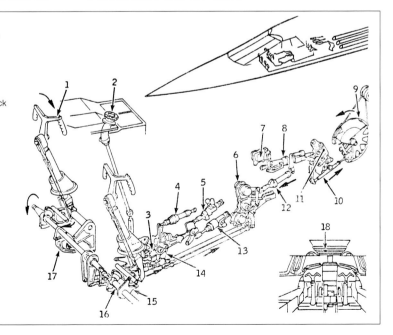

Roll Control Linkage in Fuselage

1. Control wheel
2. Trim control wheel
3. Integral trim assembly
4. Artificial feel spring rod
5. Blue artificial feel jack
6. Electrical channel synchro pack
7. AP resolver
8. Relay jack
9. Cable tension regulator
10. Jam detector strut
11. Load limiter
12. AP force limiter
13. Green artificial feel jack
14. Artificial feel input lever
15. End of travel stop
16. Pilot's torque shaft
17. Mixing limiter pitch/roll
18. 'Mech' jam warning

which the pilot's control column movements are conveyed to the hydraulic Power Control Units (PCUs) by electrical signals. The aircraft can be flown with total loss of all the electrical signals to the elevons because there is a direct link, after electrical failure, between the control column and the elevons. Under these conditions flying the aircraft is more difficult, but with practice it can be flown safely in all situations.

Conventional trim is provided in pitch, roll and yaw. An electric trim system is provided in pitch only and is controlled directly by the pilot using the pitch trim selector on each control column.

ABOVE Captain's control column and flight instruments. *Jonathan Falconer*

RIGHT Elevons in drooped, unpowered position. *Jonathan Falconer*

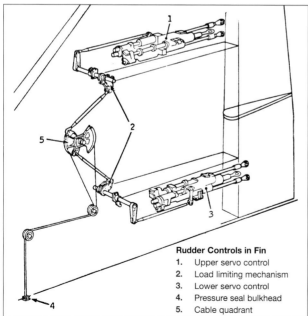

Rudder Controls in Fin
1. Upper servo control
2. Load limiting mechanism
3. Lower servo control
4. Pressure seal bulkhead
5. Cable quadrant

BELOW Twin rudders, unpowered, offset in the wind. *Jonathan Falconer*

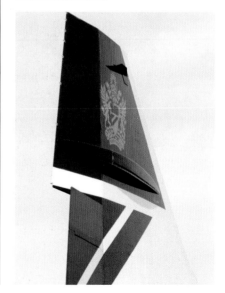

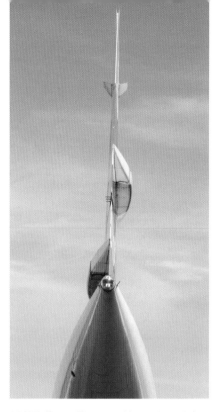

ABOVE Top and bottom rudders and both ILS localiser antennae. *Jonathan Falconer*

ABOVE Alpha Echo on maintenance at Heathrow. The escape slide built into the rear door deploys over the inner elevon. *Ian Black*

LEFT Tail unit with top rudder and ILS 2 localiser antenna. The rear baggage hold door is below. *Jonathan Falconer*

LEFT Under-wing fairings house the elevon PCUs. *Jonathan Falconer*

Chapter 3

The Power to Move

Rolls-Royce/SNECMA Olympus 593

Concorde's engines are four Rolls-Royce Olympus 593-610s, true enough, but unlike any other aircraft the term 'power plant' is more appropriate than 'engine' for the engine is but one of three elements: the intake at the front, built by BAC with a control system from BAC Guided Weapons; the engine itself; and the nozzles at the back, designed and built by SNECMA, the French aero engine company.

OPPOSITE F-WTSA at Toulouse: the starter hose along the ground is connected to the starboard nacelle ready for engine start. *Air France*

67

THE POWER TO MOVE

The engine

ABOVE AND RIGHT
Fan-jet engines like
those found on the
Airbus and Boeing
families of subsonic
aircraft have a short
round intake and a
fixed area jet pipe at
the rear; the Olympus
593 engine is fully
integrated with its
variable geometry
intake and twin
nozzles. *Ian Black/
British Airways*

First, a refresher. The motor vehicle engine, 'reciprocating engine' or 'piston engine', may be well-known to the reader. Its principal defined by the 'Otto Cycle' – induction, compression, ignition, exhaust. These four elements, popularly named 'suck, squeeze, bang, blow', occur sequentially within each cylinder, regardless of whether we consider a single-cylinder motorcycle or an 18-cylinder aero-engine.

A jet engine utilises those self-same four constituents, but now each one takes place *continuously* in its own section of the engine. Thus, suck, squeeze, bang, blow is provided by the intake, compressor(s), combustion chamber and jet-pipe/nozzle respectively. A turbine

wheel downstream of the combustion chamber extracts just enough energy from the gas-stream to drive the compressor, thus delivering continuous compression. The remaining energy exits from the propelling nozzle as thrust – the unit of measurement for jet engine power.

To complete the science lesson, the jet engine's suitability as a propulsion unit is validated by Newton's third law of motion, which states that 'for every action there is an equal and opposite reaction', whilst the broad principle of the jet engine is known as the 'Brayton Cycle'.

The Olympus had always been drawn as an axial flow, twin-spool turbojet, meaning a compressor with a straight-through flow (axial), divided into two separate sections

RIGHT Made in UK,
Fabriqué en France.
Jonathan Falconer

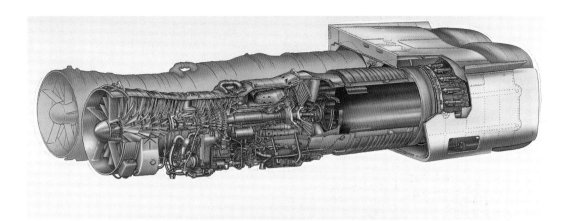

– low pressure (LP) and high pressure (HP) – each driven by its own single-stage turbine, with all the air passing through all stages of compression and on to combustion (turbojet). For a given power output, such an engine has low frontal area and high exhaust jet velocity, both of which are pre-requisites for a high-speed aircraft. Excellent as they are, a bypass or fan engine would, for the same power output, have a larger frontal area, causing too much drag and lower jet velocity – so, basically, it was no good for supersonic performance.

But the final evolution, the Olympus 593-610, had only its genes in common with its subsonic (and RAF) cousins. Initially, the model 22R engine earmarked for the RAF's BAC Tactical Strike and Reconnaissance aircraft (TSR2) was chosen. Designed for very high performance at both low level and at high altitude Mach 2 flight, its metallurgy had already been thoroughly researched – titanium for the LP compressor and the first four stages of HP compression, Nimonic 90 (a nickel, chrome, cobalt alloy) for the remaining three, and increasingly exotic nickel-based alloys for the combustion chamber and turbines.

It was during this period that the '593' line in the Olympus family tree began and straightaway gained the suffix 'D' as in Olympus 593D. Where were A, B and C one might ask? Well, it wasn't done that way: it was 'D' for Derivative, ie, an engine derived from the 22R, bench-tested to 28,800lbs of thrust, the highest power ever achieved by a turbojet anywhere in the world at that time.

Before a year was up, in the quest for guaranteed transatlantic range, the embryo SST began to grow. BSEL knew that the 593D could cope, but also knew that eating into development potential at such an early stage might not leave enough for future growth, thus the canny lads at Bristol decided on a major redesign. The 593 gained 2½ inches in diameter and 10 inches in length to accommodate larger compressors and turbines: it was designated 593B, where suffix 'B' stood for Big! And big it was, being bench-run to 32,800lbs thrust dry (without reheat), ultimately big enough for

Rolls-Royce/SNECMA Olympus 593 Mk610 turbojet

General characteristics
Type: Axial flow twin-spool turbojet with reheat
Length: 7.11m (280in)
Diameter: 1.21m (47.75in)
Dry weight: 7,000lb

Components
Compressor: Axial 7-stage low pressure, 7-stage high pressure
Combustors: Nickel alloy construction annular chamber, 16 vapourising burners, each with twin outlets
Turbine: High pressure single-stage, low pressure single-stage

Performance
Maximum Thrust: with reheat 38,050lb; without reheat 31,350lb
Overall pressure ratio: 15.5:1
Thrust to weight ratio: 5.4

the production aircraft, big enough to have 41,000lbs pencilled in for the 'B' model aircraft and beyond.

This was an engine to build on, but it was clear that still more power would be needed. Given that the very best of aerodynamic design had already been applied to compressors and turbines – they are wing-like aerofoil surfaces after all – Stage 2 tuning seeks to increase air mass flow through the engine and raise turbine entry temperature (TET).

Airflow was first addressed by adding another stage of blades to the front of the LP compressor, making seven in all. Later, an extra 5% of mass flow would be found by a re-design of the Entry Guide Vanes, in front of the LP Compressor, and a reduction in the number from seventeen to five.

At take-off condition the LP compressor, driven by a single-stage turbine, spins at 6,630rpm, creating a compression ratio of 3:1. (Note that for some years now 'rpm' gauges have been calibrated in percentage terms – 102% being the full power value for the LP spool. In operational terms LP spool speed is referred to as N1.) The LP compressor drives the Intermediate Gearbox, which itself operates the LP tachometer and provides a hand-wind connection to facilitate blade inspections by ground engineers.

OPPOSITE Olympus
being prepared for
test: the variable area
Primary Nozzle petals
and operating jacks
can be clearly seen.

The seven stages of HP compression, driven by their single-stage turbine, form the working heart of the engine. Air, at approximately 550°C, is bled from the seventh stage for the aircraft's cabin pressurisation and air conditioning systems; just upstream, at HP fifth stage, an external pipe at the top of the engine taps slightly 'less hot' air to cool the turbines and their nozzle guide vanes, and to cool and seal bearings four and five at the hot end of the engine.

Internal gearing at the front of the HP compressor connects to left-hand and right-hand accessory gearboxes which, in turn, provide drive/location for the following:

- **Left-hand** – Engine-driven fuel pump, fuel metering unit with second-stage turbo-pump co-sited, engine oil pressure pump, four scavenge pumps and filters (return oil from the bearings). Note that a magnetic chip detector sits adjacent to the LH gearbox.
- **Right-hand** – One scavenge pump, filter and magnetic chip detector, main hydraulic pump, standby hydraulic pump (engines 2 and 4 only), constant speed drive alternator, air turbine starter (as it spins during start, it drives the HP spool through the gearbox).

HP spool rpm is termed N2; at full power it turns at 105.7%, equivalent to 9,016 rpm. At

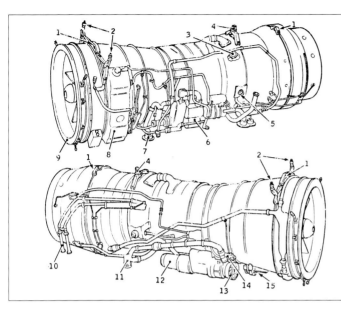

Engine Build-up Nos 1 and 3

1. Engine lifting bracket
2. Front mounts
3. Non-return valve (air conditioning)
4. Restraint spigot
5. Main mount
6. Flow meters (main and afterburning)
7. Fuel heater exhaust valve
8. Engine oil tank
9. Intake ring (aft)
10. Nozzle control pipes
11. Starter ducting
12. Integrated drive generator
13. Air starter
14. Air starter shut-off valve
15. Hydraulic connections

this speed it raises the air pressure by a further five times – a compression ratio of 5:1. Thus the two compressors working together develop a total compression ratio of 15:1.

Combustion Chamber

Air flows directly from the HP compressor to the combustion chamber where the big challenge is to separate-off exactly the right amount of air to provide the correct mixture strength for complete and efficient combustion (just like a carburettor), and to slow down that portion of air so that it doesn't keep blowing the flame out. The rest of the air – and it is a substantial amount – is a cooling medium, carefully channelled to protect the walls of the chamber from the direct heat of combustion. It is the oxygen content of this airflow that enables reheat fuel to burn in the jet pipe.

It will be recalled that Concorde prototypes generally displayed a bit of a smoky exhaust (incomplete combustion and a waste of potential thrust), but remember that the Olympus was derived from a military family of engines where function may have overridden friendliness.

Always in the plan, the cure – a totally different combustion chamber – arrived in 1970 in the penultimate evolution of the Olympus, the 593-602. Prior to this change, fuel/air mixing had taken place in eight separate but interlinked chambers. Post-modification, there was but one large annulus – a cylinder within a cylinder, if you like – and inside, sixteen twin-armed vaporisers spraying upstream against the gas flow. Rather than simply providing a highly atomised spray, the vaporisers sat far enough into the combustion chamber to be raised in temperature sufficiently to vaporise the fuel, providing highly efficient, smoke-free combustion, but extremely vulnerable to erosion, burning and cracking, alleviated to some extent by a change from fabricated to cast vaporisers.

The annular combustion chamber was initially a great success, achieving all that

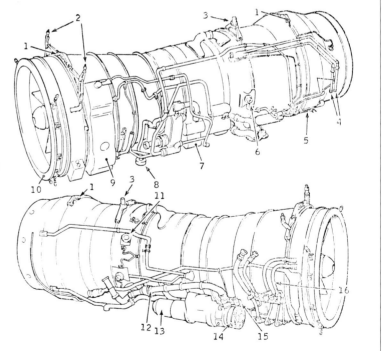

Engine Build-up Nos 2 and 4

1. Engine lifting brackets
2. Front mounts
3. Restraint
4. Nozzle control pipes
5. Signal pipes
6. Main mount
7. Flow meters (main and after burning)
8. Fuel heater exhaust valve
9. Engine oil tank
10. Intake ring (aft)
11. Non-return valve (air conditioning)
12. Air starter cross-over ducting
13. Integrated drive generator
14. Air starter
15. Air starter shut-off valve
16. Hydraulic hoses

ABOVE The engine
run-up bay in
action at Fairford,
Gloucestershire.

LEFT 'Smoky Joe's'
signature written by
the early standard
combustion chamber.
John Hamlin

was expected of it, but as engine operating hours built up after Concorde's entry into airline service, the extreme conditions within the chamber took their toll. Splits, tears, burning and erosion of the chamber walls and fractures of the fuel vaporisers were detected by borescope inspections (*see glossary*) and in-flight analysis. During this period, maintenance engineers honed their pit-stop skills to the point where a complete engine change plus the attendant ground-run test could be wrapped-up in one eight-hour shift!

Development, however, never stands still: a revised annular chamber featuring anti-corrosion ceramic plating, better cooling and more efficient combustion appeared in 1981; it was good enough to see the aeroplane out.

Turbines

And so to the turbines and the major controlling parameter – Turbine Entry Temperature.

TET has always been (and always will be) dependent upon metallurgy. Only the very best of 'superalloys' can withstand the continuous battering from the 1,000°C plus, sonic velocity gas stream. Strength, heat resistance and immunity to exotic forms of corrosion are pre-requisites. The HP turbine and its ring of guide vanes bear the brunt of this onslaught. An HP turbine blade is shown opposite. Notice the eighteen cooling holes drilled top to bottom, a technique developed to provide cooling passages for guide vanes and blades alike, using air bled from HP compressor fifth stage as the cooling medium – if 450°C air can ever be termed a cooling medium! By this means TET was raised to 1,450°C.

Turbine cooling air temperature, as a measure of turbine health, is sensed at two points between the HP and LP turbines and indicated on instruments at the flight engineer's position on the flight deck. Normal supercruise

BELOW Olympus 593-610, identifiable by its five Entry Guide Vanes. *Rolls-Royce*

A selection of damaged compressor blades (all from the HP compressor) that shows how small they get towards the end of the compressor. They display the sort of defects that would be found using the borescope for internal examination.

Turbine blade showing fir tree root, cooling holes and leading edge damage.

ABOVE The tip of a compressor blade showing a cross-section just like a wing.

RIGHT Igniter plug.

BELOW LP1 compressor blades having suffered heavy damage following ingestion of a hard object – expensive! *Piers Macdonald*

Turbine blade leading edge. Cooling holes are at the top.

value would be around 550°C, with a warning triggered at 640°C requiring an engine shut down to prevent further deterioration. Exhaust Gas Temperature (EGT) and jet pipe pressure (P7) are both measured at positions downstream of the turbines and displayed at the forward engine instruments (pilots') panel and the flight engineer's position respectively.

Ever since Frank Whittle's first jet engine, metallurgists have developed evermore complex 'recipes' in the quest for higher TET, and its attendant higher power. For example, the Olympus combustion chamber material Nimonic 263, described as nickel (47%), chromium (20%) and cobalt (20%) alloy. It has in the mix varying percentages of carbon, silicon, manganese, sulphur, aluminium, titanium, boron, copper, iron and lead with a dash of silver (0.0005%) and a hint of bismuth at 0.0001%; each element making its contribution to life in the 'hot lane'.

Oils and Bearings

The two main rotating assemblies are supported by five bearings – roller, ball, ball, roller, roller – front to rear. The LP spool has a roller bearing in front of the compressor and the thrust bearing (ball) behind, with a roller bearing to support the turbine end, whereas the shorter HP spool runs on a thrust bearing in front of the compressor and a roller in front of the turbine.

The five main bearings, together with all accessory gears and drive bearings, are lubricated by a single oil pressure pump set at 26psi. Five scavenge pumps direct return oil, through a fuel-cooled oil cooler, back to an external tank attached to the LP compressor casing, LH-side.

The oil tank contains 16 US quarts; total system content is 26 US quarts. Replenishment access is via a small hinged panel at the forward end of the main engine door; 'fill' connection and overflow connections are located at the tank base. A special hand-pump gun or dispenser must be used. There is no gravity top-up facility. For a complete oil change, oil may be drained through the 'fill' connection. Use only: Esso ETO 25; Mobil RM 193A-3; Shell ASTO 555; Royco 555; or Castrol 599.

Note that different oils must not be mixed in the same tank. Engine oil pressure, temperature and contents are displayed at the flight engineer's position.

Engine Control

The engine is controlled by a duplicated analogue electronic system, Main and Alternate, used turn and turn about. Each system can be divided into two parts: (1) the conventional fuel injection control that responds to throttle lever input to set the required fuel flow; (2) the networks that vary the primary nozzle area to control jet pipe pressure, thus matching N1 to N2.

Power Control

At the simplest level, the throttle lever sets power: its position is signalled electrically to each Engine Control Unit (ECU). The ECU mixes throttle lever position with engine and atmosperic data to output a drive to the fuel throttle valve. Additional circuits control engine acceleration and prevent exceeding maximum and minimum limits.

Mass Flow Control

Also contained within each ECU is a set of 'schedules', basically electronic graphs that output a drive signal to the primary nozzle to facilitate matching of LP and HP rpm to deliver maximum air mass flow, whilst keeping clear of surge, at all conditions. There are four 'schedules', selected either manually or automatically, according to phase of flight.

The intake

My favoured dictionary, the big Collins, allows that 'wizardry' be 'the art, skill or practice of persons outstandingly clever in some specified field'. Thus, what may have been read as an overblown metaphor is now presented as fact – the air intake in front of the Olympus engine is a piece of wizardry. There is no doubt about it. This is why.

The jet engine, as we know it, can only accept a subsonic airflow. Each of the compressor blades is of an aerofoil shape, like a wing, and, from an earlier chapter, the problems of supersonic flow over just two wings are understood only too well. But aerodynamicists in the power plant team had seen shock wave properties they could turn

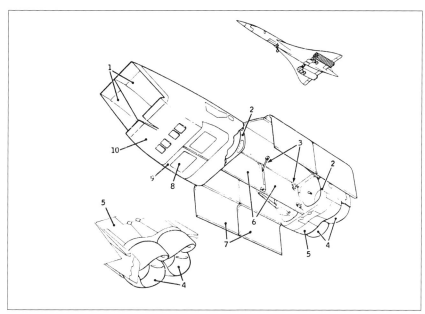

Nacelles Main Frame

1. Ramps
2. Firewall
3. Suspension links
4. Buckets
5. Exhaust structure (twin secondary nozzle structure)
6. Centre wall
7. Main access doors
8. Vane
9. Spill door
10. Intake

BELOW Left-hand intake set and 22-inch silver-coloured wheels.

ABOVE **Intake ramps.**
Jonathan Falconer

BELOW **Schematic illustration of the air intake.**

Bit by bit a viable system was built up, tested, modified and refined; striding forward upon the introduction of digital electronics, then evolving into the shape we know so well.

It is referred to as a 'two-dimensional, external compression system', for reasons that will become apparent. The other option, the variable centre-body intake (imagine the refill of a typical ball-point pen emerging from its casing, and you have it) was a non-starter, being prone to provoking noisy, violent engine surge and flame-out – coyly termed 'un-starts'.

Let's de-construct it. First the science – just a little, don't turn over!

Mr. Bernoulli, a Swiss mathematician, discovered that air flowing through a narrowing tube will increase in speed and reduce in pressure (every carburettor has used this principle to draw fuel from the float chamber). Conversely, through a widening tube the opposite occurs – the airflow reduces in speed, but increases in pressure.

to advantage. Their basic task was how to take about 1,000mph out of the airstream's speed and present a smooth and orderly airflow into the engine at Mach 0.49, all within the 11ft length of the intake – no problem there, then.

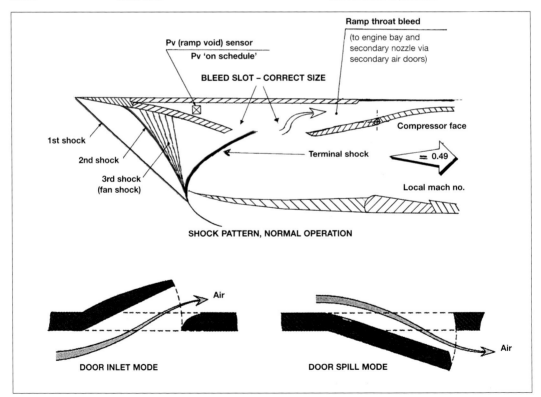

For the intake discussion we will speak not of a narrowing tube, but of a convergent duct – the same thing; similarly, a widening tube becomes a divergent duct.

Now just one more fact. Imagine the consternation when scientists discovered that at the other side of the 'sound barrier' Mr. Bernoulli's findings were turned on their head: airflow behaved in exactly the opposite manner.

However, BAC had seen something else. Supersonic airflow over an aircraft produces shock waves and they are a problem to aircraft designers. But, as a supersonic flow passes through a shock wave, it is slowed down and increased in pressure. For a power plant designer this is good, very good.

It may be worth restating at this point that the design team must slow the airflow right down from about 1,300mph to 300mph and will try to increase its pressure as much as possible – this is termed pressure recovery.

Looking at a side view of the Concorde intake, it can be seen that a convergent duct is formed by the floor of the intake and the front ramp, thus supersonic airflow through this zone will be slowed down and increased in pressure. Now the wizardry begins. Notice how the lower lip is set well back; such design promotes the growth of oblique shock waves – these being the best shape for pressure recovery.

The first shock is developed by the wedge-shaped upper lip as Mach 1.3 is approached; its angle is designed to pass just ahead of the lower lip. The second shock is generated by the front ramp hinge, whilst the third shock, a fan-shaped collection, is produced by the gently curved profile of the front ramp itself as it becomes active at Mach 1.3. The final, or terminal shock, grows from the lower lip; it performs the last element of speed reduction to subsonic flow and helps direct secondary flow up between the ramps. Note that each shock, although a powerful phenomenon, is less than 1mm thick. Thus it can be seen that shock waves are developed as a two-dimensional array, and that much of the compression takes place ahead of the lower lip in an 'external' sort of way.

The precise placement of the shock array, as shown, throughout supersonic flight, at all power settings, in all atmospheric conditions

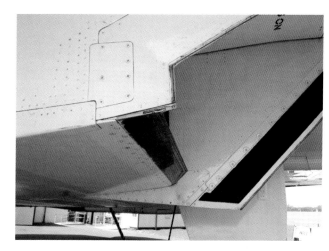

and for all aircraft manoeuvres, is absolutely crucial to power plant efficiency and smooth running. Shocks are flighty things, they will dance vigorously at the slightest change of engine power, temperature or even aircraft manoeuvres unless firmly controlled by the digital electronics or the flight engineer's fingers. Allow them to wander and airflow will distort and the engine will surge.

Having smoothly penetrated the convergent duct and its shock waves, the airflow, now safely just subsonic, finds itself in a divergent duct formed by the rear ramp and the intake floor. At last Mr. Bernoulli can take over as airflow is finally slowed to Mach 0.49 and undergoes the last element of pressure recovery to become 8½ times its starting value. In supercruise the total compression ratio from intake lip to compressor exit is 80:1! Now that's wizardry.

The conversion from theory to practise is never straightforward and commonly is fraught with compromise. In his magnum opus *Mechanics of Flight*, A.C. Kermode says 'the more one understands about aircraft, the more one realises that an aeroplane is, from beginning to end, a compromise'. Even wizards can't have things all their own way.

Many tweaks were needed to make it all work: the intakes were canted downwards and toed-in towards the aircraft centre-line to equalise airflow into each one, thereby counteracting the swept-wing effect. Precise positioning below the wing, a permanent air

ABOVE Finely tapered intake lower lip, the focus point of shock-wave development. In this zone the airflow begins its 1,000mph deceleration.
David Macdonald

Ready for business. Note how the intakes are toed-in to balance airflow into each engine during high-speed flight.

bleed from the floor of the inboard intakes, and detail changes to sidewall shape, all contributed to smooth surge-free operation.

Finally, in the last few weeks before Concorde's entry into service, it was found that No. 4 engine's first row of compressor blades were vibrating badly during take-off. Even at low speed, airflow is crucial. Here, a combination of wing flow, intake position, landing gear position and engine direction of rotation

conspired to rattle the blades. At this late stage a compromise was called for. The auxiliary vane angle was reduced and the flight engineer given an additional control to restrict No. 4 engine power until an aircraft speed of 60kts.

There remains only the spill door and secondary airflow to be considered. The spill door's job is to remain shut throughout flight, until first power reduction at deceleration point. At this stage the engine's need for air is much reduced. If the intake surfaces didn't move, the shock array would be pushed forward 'off-lip', it would become highly unstable, cause immense flow distortion and push the LP compressor into surge.

In an earlier evolution of the intake and during an initial Mach 2 exploration flight, all four engines surged at decel point throttling, causing test pilot Brian Trubshaw to declare 'that World War Three had begun', such was the racket. Thereafter, until modified units became available, speed brakes were deployed at decel point (yes, on the prototypes) and power not reduced until Mach 1.7.

But, in normal operation, as soon as power reduction is sensed, the ramps begin to lower

BELOW Engine door lower surface – vent flap; oil top-up access; manual start access rear left. *Jonathan Falconer*

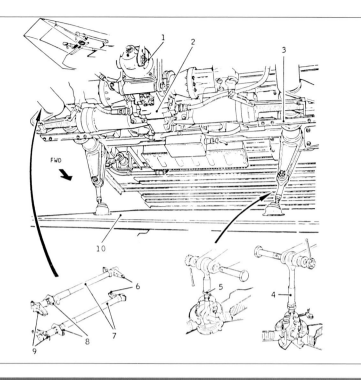

Ramp Actuation

1. Brake unit
2. Actuator
3. Centre bearing flange
4. Rear link
5. Forward link
6. Rear lever
7. Torque tube
8. Actuator lever
9. Forward lever
10. Front ramp

FWD

Engine surge

Surge is a reversal of airflow through a jet engine's compressor, usually the LP compressor. How and why does it happen? Jet engine compression is a continuous aerodynamic process using alternate rows of rotating and static aerofoil-shaped blades. Just like a wing, when airflow and aerofoil are grossly mismatched, a stall can occur – smooth flow breaks down and becomes turbulent. Inside the compressor, high pressure air downstream of the problem area finds there to be less resistance in exiting forwards (a flow reversal) than continuing rearwards. These are often rapid self-recovering, albeit noisy, events and usually non-damaging. The reasons are various: minor damage to blading, wear or even design anomalies.

In Concorde's case, although it was not a common event, engine surges were more likely to have been triggered by airflow distortion within the intake due to control system malfunction and even more rarely, by broken blading. In each case reliability modifications were put in place.

A surge would manifest itself by a series of loud

pulsing 'bumps'. Being a flow reversal, the flow distortion would spill over into the adjacent intake causing its engine to join in. Generally speaking there was no forewarning. It happened!

'It isn't possible to diagnose which one instigated the surge, therefore both engines need to be throttled to take the power out of the pulses: however, at Mach 2, it's not a good idea to pull both engines on one side down to idle – it's safe and manageable, but not a comfortable ride – therefore reduce power on all engines and begin a descent. Now select the other channels of duplicated electronic engine control and the same for intakes. This will fix it. Open up each engine in turn to cruise power and continue. Should an engine surge during open-up, cross-check engine and intake instruments again; if there is an intake anomaly, get your fingers in there to control the shock waves via the intake's manual controls, but if it's the engine, then the only option is to shut it down and continue on three – subsonically. Finally, explain it all to your passengers!'

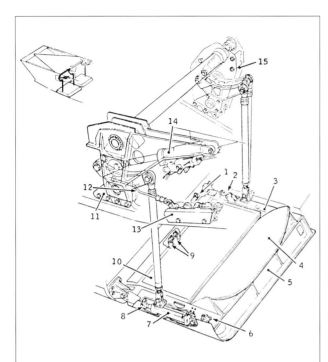

Spill Door Actuation

1. Spill door position indicator resolver
2. Vane lock mechanism
3. Centre wall box
4. De-icing mat
5. Spill door
6. Door up-stop
7. Hydraulic damper
8. Idler lever
9. Vane position indicator micro switch
10. Vane
11. Sidewall actuation mechanism
12. Connecting rod
13. Resolver chassis
14. Actuator
15. Centre wall actuation mechanism

BELOW Spill door in closed position. *David Macdonald*

to match airflow to engine need and to maintain the shocks at the correct position. Too large a ramp angle would cause unstable/uneven flow, thus for the first time, the spill door opens to dump excess air overboard. This is the only time in a flight that intake air is spilled without it having performed a useful job.

Secondary airflow is that portion of intake air ducted up through the gap between front and rear ramps, thereafter controlled by the secondary air doors. These doors, located in each corner of the intake at the nacelle interface are operated by an electric motor and cable drives. They must be closed for take-off, but are opened immediately afterwards, and they absolutely must be open to enable supersonic flight: their tasks – to provide a nacelle cooling flow and to assist the secondary nozzle in shaping the final jet efflux to squeeze out every last pound of thrust. Should a set not open, then apart from loss of efficiency, the nacelle would overheat and the engine would surge at about Mach 1.6. The electric motor was always too small, always susceptible to drive train friction, but space constraints precluded fitting anything larger. Thus, door hinges and cable drives must be maintained to an almost clinical standard of care. All operators suffered, British Airways eventually fitting an in-house designed friction monitor based on the motor's current draw, to give early warning of stiffening drives.

Nozzles

Since Concorde is the only supersonic airliner,* little of its design follows what might be called a conventional path. In the hands of the innovators, even the simple jet-pipe sprouted appendages and controls in the pursuit of performance.

There are two elements, separate yet integrated to a common purpose. The primary nozzle sits at the end of the jet-pipe. It is a ring of petals, each one operated by its own extending air-jack – rather like a bicycle pump in reverse – they operate in unison to vary the diameter, and therefore the area, of the jet pipe exit. Remember from school? The area of a circle = $\pi \times r^2$. The secondary nozzle

* The Tu-144 is acknowledged in an earlier section.

LEFT The reheat flame holder and its five stabilising fingers, with spray ring and LP turbine behind.
David Macdonald

assembly surrounds the primary, its eyelid-like doors – we call them 'buckets' – extend further aft. Together they make up another form of convergent/divergent duct.

Primary Nozzle

The primary nozzle forms the jet pipe exit. Whereas jet engines on all of the subsonic family of airliners have a fixed area jet pipe, that of the Olympus may be varied over a small range. As the jet pipe exit is made smaller (in area) the jet pipe pressure increases and has the effect of slowing down only the LP turbine and its compressor – and vice versa for a larger area. By this means the speed of the LP spool will be controlled independently of the HP spool. It is an extreme form of tuning not available to fixed jet pipe aircraft, not even the latest Airbus and Boeings. Only high performance military engines have variable nozzles.

What it means in terms of power, is that at every point of engine rpm and at every aircraft speed from start of take-off to Mach 2 and beyond, the LP compressor is accurately matched to the HP compressor for best mass airflow.

What it means in terms of power with reliability, is that at every point of temperature from the coldest atmosphere to +130°C supercruise, Turbine Entry Temperature (TET) can be maintained at its optimum level. Thus mass flow and TET parameters were addressed both in hardware design and in software architecture.

Of no lesser importance was the integration with SNECMA's reheat system. Burning fuel in the jet-pipe at the rate of 10 tonnes per hour would certainly have raised jet-pipe pressure and, much to the chagrin of Rolls-Royce, have reduced N1 had it not been for the variable area primary nozzle.

Incidentally, when testing or operating reheat, always look for a big rise on the Aj gauge (jet-pipe area) as the main indicator of reheat light-up.

Secondary Nozzle

This, the Type 28 Nozzle, is altogether a larger, more robust assembly. It has to be: fully 29% of total thrust bears on these surfaces during supercruise. Bucket drive is effected via an air motor and ball-screw jacks, operating to a mach number signal. Three completely different tasks are performed:

■ at all times below Mach 0.55 – on the ground, take-off and initial climb – the

BELOW Secondary nozzles buckets at 21°, take-off and low speed position.
Jonathan Falconer

ABOVE LEFT AND CENTRE Secondary nozzle buckets at 0° supersonic position. *David Macdonald/Jonathan Falconer*

ABOVE RIGHT Secondary nozzle bucket at reverse thrust position. *David Macdonald*

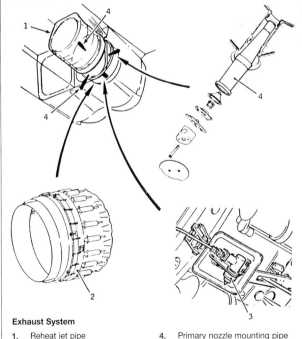

Exhaust System

1. Reheat jet pipe
2. Primary nozzle
3. Primary nozzle area transducer connector
4. Primary nozzle mounting pipe assembly

buckets are set to 21°, forming a 'jet-pump' gap at the nacelle trailing-edge. The high-speed jet exiting from the primary nozzle draws-in atmospheric air from above and below the nacelle to eradicate a source of drag (base drag) that would otherwise exist between the nozzles.

- once the secondary air doors have opened and a strong secondary flow established, base drag no longer exists, thus the buckets are opened progressively to 0° by Mach 1.1, to form a divergent duct. The fully established secondary flow and buckets at 0° work together to shape and control the jet efflux, to optimise thrust in supersonic flight.

- for reverse thrust on landing, the buckets close across the jet-pipe deflecting exhaust flow forwards. The inboard engines may be set to idle reverse in flight to increase rate of descent.

Engine health monitoring

The Olympus 593-610 was a tough, hard-working engine, yet so highly tuned as to squeeze every last ounce of efficiency from it. It was unique. There was nothing to compare it with; there was nothing to compare with it.

In-service reliability was good – very good: not many aircraft are sent round the world on four-week itineraries. But there was a work-load – to monitor engine health, to intercept a problem before it arose, preventive maintenance, and it was broken down into five headings: SOAP, MCD, EGT, oil consumption and borescope.

SOAP – Spectrographic Oil Analysis Programme

Every 50 flying hours oil samples are taken from each engine, at Heathrow, within 2 hours of shut-down and before replenishment. Samples were dispatched on a daily run to a company at Fairoaks in Surrey for same-day laboratory analysis. Initially, the samples were scanned for traces of iron, magnesium and silicon, the units of measurement being parts per million (ppm). Should any of these elements reach 'alert level' then an additional search was made for nickel, chrome and aluminium. Should Iron exceed its alert level by a particular amount, then the Magnetic Chip Detectors (MCD) were analysed and considered in conjunction with the spectro results before the engine could continue in service. Whenever an alert was met, a recurring requirement was raised directing a spectro and MCD check at every return to base. Thus critical decisions on engine serviceability used both sets of evidence.

MCD – Magnetic Chip Detectors

Whereas my 2CV engine had one magnetic probe built into the sump, the Olympus had three Magnetic Chip Detectors and a specialist group to analyse them. The three MCDs were strategically placed within the engine as follows:

- in the left-hand gearbox scavenge filter specifically trapping debris from the thrust bearings (2 and 3) and the left-hand gearbox.
- in the right-hand gearbox scavenge filter, trapping debris generated within the right-hand gearbox.
- in the main external return-flow pipe. This one designated 'Master MCD'; it attracted debris from the total system.

Every Service Check – 175 flying hours – all three MCDs were removed for deposit analysis. 'Big lumps' went under the microscope for shape and form assessment; a rolled flaky appearance was indicative of a bearing problem, while a more granular particle

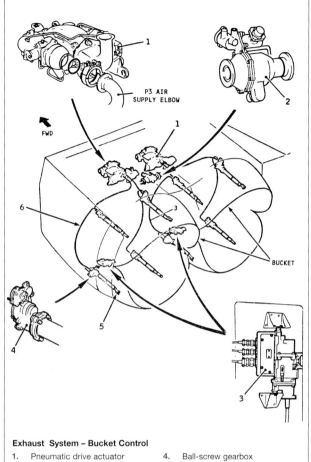

P3 AIR SUPPLY ELBOW

FWD

BUCKET

Exhaust System – Bucket Control

1.	Pneumatic drive actuator	4.	Ball-screw gearbox
2.	Cross-feed isolation valve	5.	Flexible shaft
3.	Bucket position transmitter (indicator)		

suggested gear or shaft frettage. But it's the sludge that was fascinating. To put it another way, reading the tea leaves was finished – the real message was in the ring around the rim.

The sludge sample was bombarded with X-rays. Each chemical element in the amalgam would emit a different radiation. Using a computer, programmed with the radiation signatures of elements used in engine metals, the analyst would be presented with a readout of the detailed composition of the sludge. Moving on a step further, knowing exactly what each engine alloy was made of, and introducing

Reheat

The engine was optimised, in size and
performance, for supercruise – low drag,
high efficiency, no compromise. At take-off,
dry power (full throttle, but without reheat) is
31,000lbs; reheat is a simple, lightweight method
of raising total thrust to the requisite 38,050lbs.

**Reheat Fuel Injection
System**

1. Mounting rods
2. Flame holder
3. Anvil
4. Spray ring
5. Reheat flame
   detector
6. Reheat igniter
7. Fuel connection
8. Jet pipe
   thermocouple

INNER CONE

The system, connected to the engine fuel
supply, comprises a single spray ring and
flame holder mounted on the tail cone behind
the turbines. Fuel, metered electronically in
proportion to engine fuel flow, is switched
from the flight deck. When the system is
activated, fuel flows to the ring, is sprayed
upstream into the gas flow and is lit by a
timed run of a single igniter plug. The flame
then stabilises on the flame holder, some
8 inches behind the ring. Utilising residual
oxygen in the gas flow, its effect is to further
increase jet velocity, adding approximately
22% of thrust at take-off and 30% at
climb power for transonic acceleration. Its
performance is monitored on the flight deck,
first by noting rise in fuel flow at initiation,
followed by indication of primary nozzle area
running fully open on light-up.

Reheat is used on every take-off, its
light-up sequence taking place on the roll as
the engine accelerates up to full power – it
needs the mass flow associated with an N1
of 81% or more to function. It is switched
off at 500ft on a standard flight or at noise
abatement cut-back where needed. For
the transonic acceleration it is switched on
at climb power at M0.95, then off again at
M1.7 – a run of between 10 and 15 minutes
dependent upon aircraft weight and outside
air temperature.

graphics, the sample's footprint could be compared with known footprints: eg, No. 1 bearing housing was made from an iron-based alloy, MSRR 6544 – in addition to its base material it had 25% carbon, 14% chrome, 1% manganese, 1% nickel and 0.8% silicon. Having matched the footprint, one could point fairly precisely to the assembly under suspicion.

It was well known that a newly installed engine would generate a relatively high level of debris as shafts, gears and bearings bedded-in and greases, used in engine build, washed down – grease raises the silicon content. Nevertheless, the checks remained. An engine must demonstrate three consecutive good checks before removal from the 'alert' file.

Exhaust Gas Temperature (EGT) Trend

The combustion chamber, even in its latest incarnation, still took a battering from the high energy gas flow. Deterioration, before becoming damage would still upset temperature patterns, and to catch a trend before it became a problem had huge benefits.

In 1986 Rolls-Royce devised an EGT trend analysis program to be loaded into a programmable Sharp 1248 hand-held calculator.

This became a routine part of the flight engineer's in-flight tasks. Using real-time data, even the smallest divergence of EGT was apparent; recording and plotting created the trend. Its *raison d'être*, a rising trend was indicative of a problem within the combustion chamber/turbine area – cooling holes unzipping, vaporiser cracking, hot streaking – 20C° up would result in a borescope internal inspection upon return to base. A dynamically increasing trend would require a shut-down judgement. A minor reducing trend would result from compressor deterioration (nicks, scratches, erosion etc). Cruise EGT, incidentally would be about 650°C.

Oil Consumption

At each station, oil uplift and flight time were assessed to produce a consumption rate; once again recorded and plotted so that trends were immediately apparent.

Borescope

The medical people call it an endoscope. It's the same miniaturised viewing technology. Engines are designed with inspection ports in key areas, blanked-off in service, but readily available for either routine internal inspections or 'alert level' extras when SOAP, MCD or EGT require.

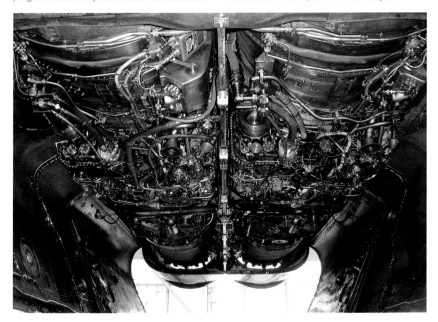

LEFT A tight fit. Red hoses are hydraulic pipes; left-hand oil tank to the front; right-hand starter adjacent to the three hydraulic hoses. *Allan Burney*

Chapter 4

Flightdeck

It's quite an office. Once in the seats it fits like a glove; getting there a little more difficult – bend low, don't damage the equipment on the overhead panel then stride carefully over the centre console. Seats are electrically powered, a must during high pitch-attitude flight. Instrumentation is conventional for the period, a wealth of information displayed full-time. It was a wonderful environment – compact, purposeful, more of a 'cockpit' than flightdeck. A pleasure to have worked in, a pleasure to have shared with our travelling public.

OPPOSITE Concorde flightdeck – pilots' controls and instruments. *PRM Aviation*

Pilots' dash panels and consoles

Captain's dash panel

1. Instrument transfer switches
2. Airspeed indicator
3. Mach meter
4. Warning and landing display – autoflight
5. Attitude director indicator (artificial horizon)
6. Vertical speed indicator 1,000ft/min scale
7. Radio altimeter (ft above ground)
8. Radio navigation annunciator lights
9. Altimeter
10. Failure and comparator lights
11. Clock: GMT/elapsed time/ countdown timer
12. Standby artificial horizon
13. Radio marker beacon lights – airways and approach
14. Engine rating lights
15. Centre of gravity indicator (CG)
16. Standby altimeter
17. Triple temperature indicator: total – static – deviation
18. Medium Frequency (MF) radio compass (ADF)
19. Flight director data change-over switch (FD1/FD2)
20. Side slip indicator
21. Horizontal situation indicator (HSI) – compass
22. VHF radio compass VOR 1 and 2 – two pointers on compass card
23. Standby airspeed indicator/Mach meter
24. DME indicators (distance measuring equipment)
25. Incidence/G meter

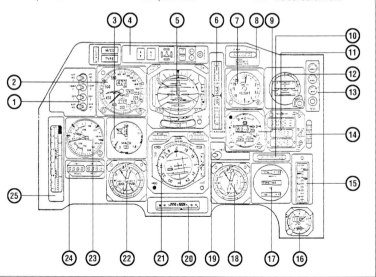

First officer's dash panel

1. Visor/nose control lever
2. Visor position indicator
3. Windscreen wipers normal/override selector
4. Landing gear and tyre deflation W/L
5. Air speed indicator
6. Mach meter
7. Warning and landing display – autoflight
8. Artificial horizon
9. Vertical speed indicator 1,000ft/min scale
10. Radio navigation annunciator lights
11. Radio altimeter (ft above ground)
12. Instrument transfer switches
13. Radio marker beacon lights (airways and approach)
14. Clock: GMT and countdown timer
15. –
16. Total temperature indicator: static – deviation
17. Altimeter
18. Medium Frequency (MF) radio compass (ADF)
19. Flight director data changeover switch (FD1/FD2)
20. Side slip indicator
21. Horizontal situation indicator (HSI) – compass
22. VHF radio compass VOR 1 and 2 – two pointers on compass card
23. DME indicators
24. Normal brakes – anti-skid annunciator panel
25. Landing gear safety baulk override
26. Landing gear control lever
27. Flying controls position and control channel indicator (ICOVOL)
28. Landing gear position indicator lights
29. Wheel light – ON indicates brakes > 270°C or tyre deflation

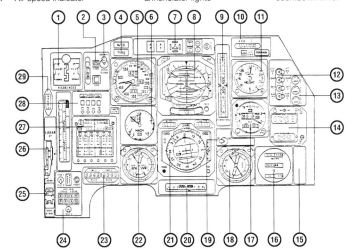

FAR RIGHT Visor/nose control lever.
Jonathan Falconer

RIGHT The Icovol flight controls position indicator.
Jonathan Falconer

RIGHT Automatic Flight Control System (AFCS) panel, which includes dual auto throttles, autopilots and flight directors.
David Macdonald

Glare shield panel autopilot controls

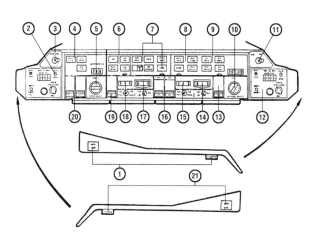

1. Co-pilot's autoland warning light and steering fail light
2. VOR/ILS frequency selector
3. Radio/INS selector switch
4. Auto-throttle mode selection
5. Auto-throttle speed selection
6. Autopilot horizontal mode select
7. Autoland engage push button
8. Autopilot vertical mode push buttons
9. Autopilot vertical (altitude) push button
10. Autopilot 'altitude to fly' selector
11. Radio/INS switch
12. VOR/ILS frequency selector
13. No 2 flight director engage switch
14. No 2 VOR/localiser course selector
15. No 2 heading pull/track push selector window
16. Autopilot 1 or 2 engage switches
17. No 1 localiser selector
18. Heading track selector
19. Flight director No 1 engage switch
20. Autothrottles 1 and 2 engage switch
21. Captain's autoland warning light and steering failure

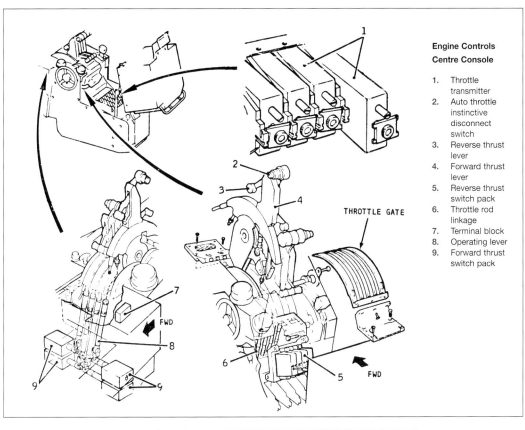

Engine Controls Centre Console

1. Throttle transmitter
2. Auto throttle instinctive disconnect switch
3. Reverse thrust lever
4. Forward thrust lever
5. Reverse thrust switch pack
6. Throttle rod linkage
7. Terminal block
8. Operating lever
9. Forward thrust switch pack

THROTTLE GATE

FWD

FWD

LEFT Engine throttle levers with reverse levers ahead and white 'piano-key' reheat selectors behind. Note the throttle lever extensions to assist the shorter-armed flight engineer.
Jonathan Falconer

Centre console (forward)

1. No 1 INS navigation computer (CDU)
2. No 2 INS navigation computer (CDU)
3. Cabin altitude gauge
4. Captain's and co-pilot's audio select panel (comms/nav/PA/intercom)
5. Selcal: indication, ATC, call (mainly HF)
6. Autopilot datum adjust turn control

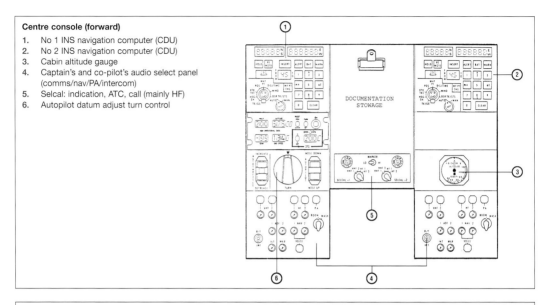

Centre console (aft)

1. Trim controls
2. Engine throttles
3. Rain repellent push-button (system withdrawn)
4. Nose/visor standby control
5. Reheat selectors
6. Throttle warning lights (failure of engine electrical control system)
7. Brake system selector lever
8. No 3 INS navigation control and display unit
9. HF communications radio control panel
10. Lights, brightness and test selector
11. Air data computer controls
12. Landing gear standby lowering lever
13. ADF navigation receivers control panel
14. ATC transponders control panel
15. Weather radars control panel
16. VHF communications radio control panel

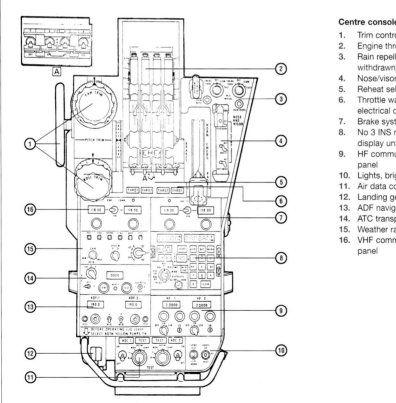

LEFT Centre dash
panel instruments.
Jonathan Falconer

Centre dash panel

1. Exhaust primary nozzle size (% area)
2. Exhaust gas temperature (EGT) x 100°C
3. Fuel flow 1,000kg/hr (engine + reheat)
4. Engine N1 LP compressor speed (% rpm)
5. Engine N2 HP compressor speed (% rpm)
6. Engine indicator lights. Green=GO;
   Amber=CONFIGURATION; Blue=REVERSE
7. Dual brake pressure gauge: LH and RH wheels
   emergency/parking pressures
8. Brake failure warning lights, upper: normal
   brakes low pressure warning; lower: brake
   selector lever 'not at normal' advisory
9. Take-off monitor
10. Autoflight panel illumination control
11. Fuel contents indicator

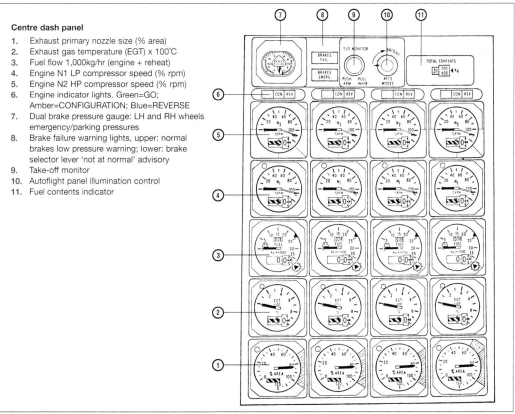

1. Master warning system
2. Windshield electrical de-ice indicators
3. Main landing lights switches
4. Flight control invertors panel
5. No 1 autostabs engage switches – pitch, roll and yaw
6. No 1 artificial feel engage switches – pitch, roll and yaw
7. Nos 1, 2, 3 and 4 engine shut down handles (four)
8. Engine fire extinguisher 1st shot
9. Engine fire extinguisher 2nd shot
10. Fire flaps light (indicates all engine-bay vent flaps shut during engine fire drill)
11. Nos 1 and 2 electric pitch trim engage switches
12. No 2 artificial feel engage switches – pitch, roll and yaw
13. Audio warning cancel push button
14. No 2 autostabs engage switches – pitch, roll and yaw
15. Anti-stall systems panel
16. Taxi-turn light switches
17. Secondary landing light switches
18. Outer and middle elevons, inner elevons, rudders mode selectors
19. Flight deck glazing de-ice switches

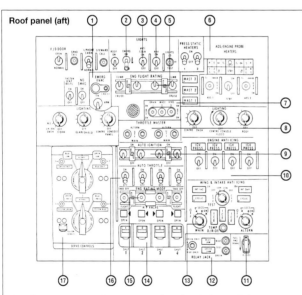

Roof panel (aft)

1. Emergency evacuation warning control
2. Emergency lights selector
3. Anti-collision lights switch
4. Navigation lights switch
5. Engine flight rating switches
6. Air data sensors heater switches
7. Water drain mast heater switches
8. Throttle master switches (engine electrical control)
9. Auto ignition switches
10. Engine anti-ice panel
11. Emergency fuel-forward-transfer switch
12. Flight control relay jacks
13. Wing and intake anti-icing panel
14. Fuel system HP valves
15. Engine rating mode switches
16. Auto throttle master switches
17. Flight controls hydraulic supply panel

BELOW Roof panel controls. *Allan Burney*

ABOVE Throttle lever angle bug (arrowed).
Jonathan Falconer

LEFT Co-pilot's seat. *Jonathan Falconer*

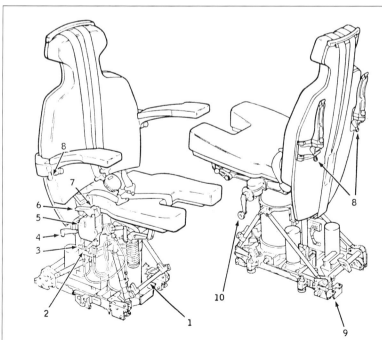

Captain's Seat and Controls

1. Micro switch actuating cam
2. Seat pan lock release lever
3. Seat back lock release lever
4. Emergency crash lock and motor drive disconnect lever
5. Seat height control switches
6. Crash lock release lever
7. Fore and aft control switches
8. Armrest release lever
9. Rear proximity switch
10. Seat height manual adjustment handle

1 Visor gold-film heating strips and their patch-like temperature sensors. *Jonathan Falconer*

2 Landing gear normal control lever. *Jonathan Falconer*

3 Vertical speed indicator. *Jonathan Falconer*

4 Rudder pedals with left and right brakes pedals at top. *Jonathan Falconer*

5 Mach meter. *Jonathan Falconer*

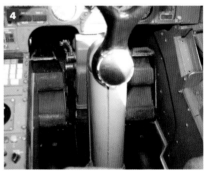

Flight engineer's panels

RIGHT Flight engineer station.

BELOW Flight engineer's seat.

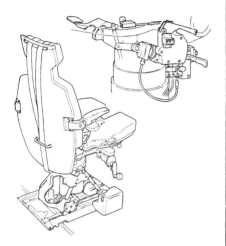

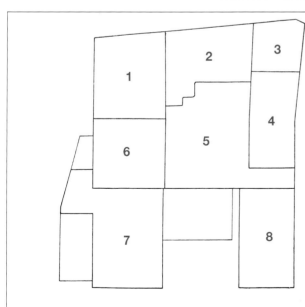

Instrument Locator for Flight Engineer's Panels

1. Left Top Panel – brake pressure and temp, cabin pressure control, engine control schedule
2. Centre Top Panel – engine air bleed, temp control, equipment bay cooling
3. Hydraulic Management Panel
4. Electrical Control Panel
5. Fuel Management and Fuel Pressurisation Panels
6. Air Intakes and Engine Secondary Instruments Panels
7. Forward Leg Panel – engine start, fuel vent, fire sensors, lighting, door and landing gear faults, ram air turbine, de-icing
8. Aft Leg Panel – fire detection and control, crew and passenger oxygen, compass

ABOVE Air conditioning bleed control and temperature control panel. *David Macdonald*

RIGHT Intake control panel. *David Macdonald*

FAR RIGHT Engine secondary instruments. Note that No. 3 engine oil system has been temporarily modified to reduce oil pressure to minimise consumption. *David Macdonald*

Chapter 5

The Pilot's View

David Leney

David Leney joined BOAC in 1956, navigating Argonauts and Constellations, before becoming a co-pilot on Britannia and VC10 aircraft. His command on the VC10 came in 1971 and he joined the Concorde fleet in 1977 as a pilot. David retired from British Airways as Captain and Flight Manager in 1989, becoming a co-pilot for two extra years. He achieved 5,000 flying hours on Concorde.

OPPOSITE Central to the pilots' instrument panel, this section presents the four Olympus engines' performance data. Note visor/nose lever at top right, landing gear selector at lower right and centre of gravity instrument at far left. *David Macdonald*

103
THE PILOT'S VIEW

As a captain I always looked forward to going to work on Concorde. The beauty of it being only a small fleet (seven aircraft in total) was that you nearly always knew other flight members, be they flight or cabin crew. For ten years we flew together as a group until command opportunities for senior co-pilots became available on other fleets. Although it was not planned as such, these were ideal conditions for the introduction of a radically different aircraft like Concorde.

The flight crew met at Tech Block A – known as TBA in those days – and we were driven to the Queen's Building for briefing, checking fuel flight plan and route and terminal weather. We drove out to the aircraft to meet the ground crew and ground engineers, several of whom we had also got to know. Up the steps on to the flight deck and into my seat – the all-singing all-dancing seat which moved electrically to any position I wanted.

The co-pilot and I began our 'scan' checks. We quietly and separately checked everything on our sides of the flight deck, and then we were joined by the flight engineer who, by now, had completed his external checks. The fuel was now on board.

Time permitting I would to go into the terminal building to meet the passengers and give them details of the flight – 3 hours 22 minutes to JFK. We also knew some of them who were regular travellers with us. We were all one happy family!

Engine start–up procedure

Pre-flight checks are defined in the *Flight Crew Operating Manual*. The flight engineer will carry out a specific set of actions concerned with the application of ground electrics to the aircraft followed by an external inspection. Each crew member then 'scans' his own panel, setting controls and testing as required. When all are ready the co-pilot will read the Before Start Check. During checklist work, 'C' = Captain, 'P' = Co-pilot, 'E' = Flight Engineer and 'G' = Ground Engineer.

1   **Throttles idle.**

2   **Anti-collision lights on.**

3 Throttle Masters on.

4 Engine feed pumps on.

5 Cross-bleed open, start pressure checked.

6 Debow switches on.

7 Start valve open.

8 HP valve open.

9 Light-up – EGT indicator.

10 Oil pressure registers.

11 Hydraulics on.

12 Electrics on.

13 Air-conditioning on.

All start-up procedure photos courtesy Jonathan Falconer

14 Low idle selected.

15 Brake fans on.

Soon two of the four engines are started, I selected 'visor down' and we are cleared to push-back and to start the other two engines. Taxi clearance, nose to 5° and proceed slowly out towards runway 27R.

Considerable power (up to 80% N2) may be required to start moving when at heavy weight. Once moving, idle power is ample. A few smooth brake applications are preferable to continuous braking to avoid high brake temperatures.

The pilots' position is 38ft in front of the nose wheel and 97ft from the main wheels, therefore great care should be taken to keep main wheels on the taxiway during turns. A look out of the open DV (direct vision) windows should be made if there is any doubt (all wheels and wing-tip can then be seen).

I remember one occasion at an air display when the flight deck was immediately above the crowd standing by the taxiway during a right-angle turn. The noise must have been horrendous and there were several frightened faces looking up at me.

BELOW **A massive double-ended aircraft tug eases 186 tonnes of Concorde off the gate.** *Ian Black*

ABOVE CG position.
Jonathan Falconer

ABOVE RIGHT
Transfer pumps on.
Jonathan Falconer

RIGHT Steering tiller
– captain's side, the
co-pilot's is similar.
Jonathan Falconer

FAR RIGHT DV
window shut.
Jonathan Falconer

RIGHT London-
Heathrow: 'Concorde
001, cleared to line-up,
27R.' *David Macdonald*

The fuel allowed for taxiing at Heathrow was 1,400kgs so any delay for take-off was to be avoided if possible.

I call, 'Before take-off check, please'.

We are cleared by Heathrow Tower on to the runway and line up. 'Concorde 1 is cleared for take-off.'

'Everyone ready? 3–2–1–now!' We all press our stop-watches at the same time; I quickly push open the throttles and Concorde's engines

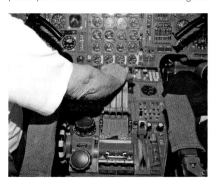

ABOVE Joining the runway. *Ian Black*

LEFT Top to bottom: N2 rpm, N1 rpm, fuel flow including reheat, exhaust gas temperature and primary nozzle area. Notice the yellow '4' – the 'reheats required' indicator; a simple piece of bent tin as an aide memoire for whether 3 or 4 reheats are needed for take-off. *Jonathan Falconer*

FAR LEFT Throttles are pushed to the stops. *Jonathan Falconer*

wind up to full power and she moves down the
runway faster and faster.

The co-pilot calls: '100kts – 4 Greens – V1.'
Above V1 we are committed to take-off come
what may. I transfer my right hand from the
throttles to the control column and the throttles
are now handled by the engineer.

The co-pilot calls 'Rotate'. I then gently pull
back the control column to achieve an attitude
of 13½°. 'V2 – positive climb.'

I call 'Gear up'. 250kts is achieved.

ABOVE Pitch attitude. *David Macdonald*

RIGHT *Son et lumière*! *Ian Black*

Reduced noise take-off

Opposition from environmental and residents' groups to Concorde's noise, particularly on the Eastern Seaboard of the United States, stimulated much political debate on both sides of the Atlantic. It led to the introduction of a general noise abatement protocol for aircraft flying into and out of John F. Kennedy Airport in New York. Ironically, Concorde was actually quieter than many expected – and quieter, certainly, than a number of aircraft then in airline service, like the Boeing 707 and 727.

For Concorde, Runway 31L at New York John F. Kennedy Airport was the best runway for take-offs in normal conditions from the noise point of view. New York ATC was very co-operative and allowed Concorde to use a runway other than the one in use for subsonic air traffic.

Take-off from 31L required a left-turn to proceed over Jamaica Bay on the south western tip of Long Island, avoiding Hamilton Beach and Howard Beach in the New York City borough of Queens. Because of Concorde's greater speed the turn was made earlier than with other aircraft, so the procedure had to be effective and safe. Much practice on the flight simulator was carried out to achieve the best possible procedure in all conditions and taking into account any unexpected failures. Further 'live' practice took place at RAF Brize Norton with the aircraft itself. The FAA and BAC had noise monitors installed everywhere to ensure that Concorde was really acceptable to all communities.

The procedure used

The '31L technique' that finally emerged can be divided into four stages: rotate to O2 (typically 13%) at 2½° per second and stabilise with wings level, turn left, once established at O2 and a rate of climb of 500ft/min (fpm) has been achieved, using 25° of bank (achieved in 6 seconds) while maintaining O2 .

At 4 seconds to the calculated Noise Time the co-pilot calls '3–2–1–noise'. At 'noise' the flight engineer simultaneously switches off reheat and brings the throttles rapidly back to the calculated TLA. That takes care of the communities near the airfield.

To achieve ATC's height requirements, on passing a heading of 235° (no longer heading towards the communities) increase to climb power. Maintain 250kt, reduce bank to 7½° (reducing bank increases climb performance). ATC's height requirement is now met but Concorde is approaching the community on the Rockaway Peninsula. So, crossing the 253 radial from the JFK VOR power is again reduced to the noise abatement TLA. Once clear of that last community and over the sea Concorde can really get underway. On reaching 5nm from the Canarsie radio beacon, slowly increase to climb power over 10 seconds.

One result of the Concorde noise abatement procedure was that other aircraft were forced to tighten up theirs, because ours was producing less noise. Therefore Concorde made New York a little quieter!

ABOVE Reheat off – controlled from the four 'piano-key' selectors behind the throttles. *Jonathan Falconer*

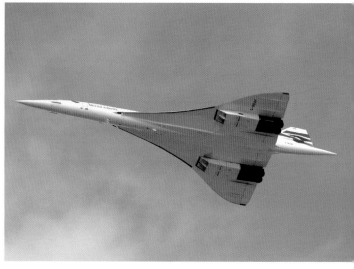

ABOVE Gear up, nose and visor up. We're on our way. *Ian Black*

'3–2–1–noise' calls the co-pilot. The engineer officer switches off the reheats and pulls back the throttles rapidly to 'Noise Power' and 250kts is maintained. We cross Woodley Beacon above 4,000ft and the noise abatement procedure is complete. We are cleared to 28,000ft and to cruise at Mach 0.95. Auto pilot is engaged – 29,000ft primed on the AFCS (Automatic Flight Control System).

Time now to talk on the PA and brief the passengers for the acceleration through Mach 1 (the speed of sound), explaining how we do it and what they will feel. Re-heats are switched on two at a time, and with two small pushes in the back we are supersonic and climbing. There is no

LEFT Climb power selected – throttles still on the stops. *Jonathan Falconer*

FAR LEFT Fuel check: 'TOTAL CONTENTS' adds the 13 tanks' contents; 'TOTAL FUEL REM' subtracts fuel used from the start quantity. *Jonathan Falconer*

LEFT Trim transfer and CG shift begin. *Jonathan Falconer*

RIGHT The intake pressure ratio gauges. *Jonathan Falconer*

FAR RIGHT TOP Exhaust Gas Temperature gauges (EGT), sensed at positions behind the turbines. *Jonathan Falconer*

FAR RIGHT BOTTOM The Icovol (flight control position indicator) is a precision instrument calibrated in degrees: six elevon and two rudder dumb-bell-shaped indicators. Coloured 'flags' indicate whether in Blue, Green or Mechanical flight control signalling. *Jonathan Falconer*

Reduced noise approach

Lack of a suitable engine is the main reason for the lack of a second generation SST. It is a conundrum. Take all the constituent parts – they can be assembled into an engine of a suitable power and one of a suitable dimension, but not into an engine that could match the attenuated noise levels of the big fans.

Some level of noise reduction during initial climb-out was provided by the nozzles. Secondary nozzle buckets at 21° reduced drag and improved climb-to-height over nearby communities. Primary nozzle at its widest, at noise abatement cut-back, enabled more mass-flow and a lower power setting. Similarly for approach, there was an optimum primary nozzle position that gave a good mass-flow but kept clear of surge.

The principle of noise abatement departures was well understood, but what about noise abatement arrivals? Enter the 'decelerating approach', a term that would not have found favour among operators 30 years ago, a period when much emphasis was placed on 'the stable approach' (ie, speed stable, gear down, landing flap by 1,500ft). However, Concorde's controllability made it entirely practical. Concorde's range of approach speeds that were beyond minimum drag speed made it desirable. (That is, during approach phase, each speed reduction required more power to hold the speed, not less.) And so the decelerating approach, also known as 'Reduced Noise Approach', became the standard whenever glide-slope guidance from the runway's Instrument Landing System (ILS) was available.

This is how it worked: final approach was flown at 190kts down to 800ft, hence the '800' height call. At 800ft the Auto Throttle system was commanded to capture Vref +7kts. Power was thus reduced to allow for a deceleration, thereby enabling the aircraft to fly over close-in communities at significantly lower noise. At approximately 500ft the power came up gently to hold Vref +7.

All benefits derive from the fact that a higher speed is flown at a lower angle-of-attack, is therefore subject to less drag and thus uses less power and makes less noise.

Since less power also meant less fuel and less time, it is tempting to describe the Reduced Noise Approach as a win, win, win situation, but there was a slight penalty. Increased touchdown speed meant more brake wear, but that was a small price to pay for good community relations.

FAR LEFT Elevon electric pitch trim control; the autopilot disconnect push button is beneath. *Jonathan Falconer*

LEFT The 'Marilake' displays – Mach number, altitude, mph, temperature and distance to go. *Jonathan Falconer*

FAR LEFT 'Yes please!' A glass of champagne at Mach 1.5. *Antony Loveless*

LEFT Lunch preparation. There is always a choice of three main dishes. *Associated Press*

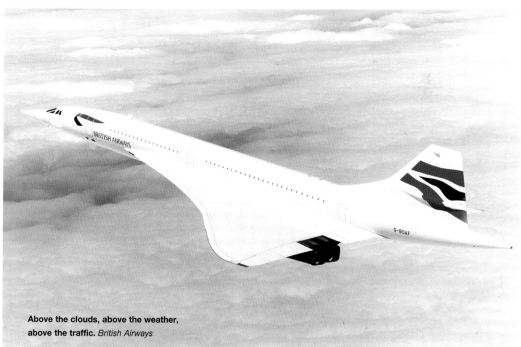

Above the clouds, above the weather, above the traffic. *British Airways*

ABOVE Short finals – 220ft. *David Macdonald*

ABOVE Nose gear still in the air. *David Macdonald*

BELOW All wheels on. *David Macdonald*

BELOW Captain Dave Leney exits the runway.

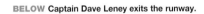

sensation at Mach 1 at all – a sobering thought is that in the past airmen have died during the exploration of transonic flight. That the aircraft passed Mach 1 without a murmur is a testament to the designers' skill. At Mach 1.3 I cannot resist a glance over my right shoulder to see the engine intakes move and begin managing the airflow throughout the rest of supersonic flight. At Mach 1.7 the reheats are switched off.

When we reach Mach 2 at 50,000ft I tell the passengers 'Mach 2 is 1,320mph – 22 miles per minute, one mile in 2¾ seconds. That is Concorde.'

The cabin crew serves cocktails and we have already had a cup of tea. They really do work hard, serving cocktails and a main meal, coffee and liqueurs for up to 100 very discerning passengers. They also serve us a meal on the flight deck. For safety reasons the two pilots cannot eat the same meal in case one of us gets ill.

Passengers set their watches to New York time – 5 hours back from GMT, then they realise that they are to arrive at 9.30am, having left London at 10.30am!

The flight engineer obtains the Eastern Seaboard weather and all is well – no delays. I can now invite passengers up to look at the flight deck. This is a great pleasure as they are always interested and enthusiastic. Over the years I have met many famous people from film, theatre, sport and business.

Having achieved 57,000ft it is now time to consider the deceleration and descent. We must be subsonic at a certain distance from Long Island to prevent a sonic boom from reaching land, so I give a thorough briefing to the others. At a pre-calculated point, power is gently reduced, deceleration begins and then descent to 39,000ft – back into the realm of the Jumbo.

New York is always pretty busy in the air but 9.00am is a good time to land and we are soon cleared by air-traffic control to join the ILS (instrument landing system) for Runway 22R. I brief the crew for a Reduced Noise Approach. At 1,500ft I call, 'Gear down and landing check'.

The speed is 190kts and 157kts is dialled in the Auto Throttle Acquire window. (157kts is the threshold speed plus 7kts.)

The co-pilot calls '800ft' and the 'AT ACQUIRE' is pressed to decelerate to 157kts. At 500ft the power increases slightly to maintain

157kts. At 40ft I disconnect the AT but maintain power. I can feel the aircraft settling into the ground effect (air trapped between the big delta wing and the runway surface), which tends to tip the aircraft nose-down and so I pull back on the control column to hold pitch attitude constant.

At 15ft, sitting in ground effect and in the vertical component of thrust, I ease back the power to idle, holding attitude as the aircraft settles gently onto the runway.

I select Idle Reverse on the engines and then land the nose wheel, push forward on the stick selecting Full Reverse power and the eight carbon fibre brakes give a reassuring deceleration from 185mph down to a taxi-speed below 20mph.

There is always a feeling of immense satisfaction on arrival.

ABOVE 'Five greens, clear to land' – one green for each gear and one for the nose. *Ian Black*

BELOW One sixty-four knots over the fence and into ground effect. *Ian Black*

Chasing the Eclipse – Roger Mills, Concorde Captain, 1987–2000

On 11 August 1999 a total eclipse of the sun was due to take place. It would be visible over central Europe across a narrow track through south west England, northern France, southern Belgium and Germany, Austria, Hungary, northeast Yugoslavia, southern Romania, the extreme north of Bulgaria, the Black Sea and Turkey. The greatest period of totality would be in Romania and totality would take place in two European capitals, Luxembourg and Bucharest. In Britain the track would cross the Scilly Isles, Cornwall, Devon and the Island of Alderney.

Goodwood Travel, a regular charterer of Concorde, put forward a proposal to fly two Concordes into mid-Atlantic then return along the track of totality, giving their passengers an extended view of the eclipse. Sounds simple doesn't it? However, before we proceeded there were many questions to be answered. The experience of British Aerospace at Filton was drawn upon to answer some of these questions.

Concorde 001 commanded by André Turcat had chased an eclipse from Las Palmas to Fort Lamy (now Ndjamena), Chad, on the 30 June 1973. For that exercise 001 had been fitted with special observing equipment and five windows in the top of the fuselage. Would our passengers be able to observe the eclipse from the normal

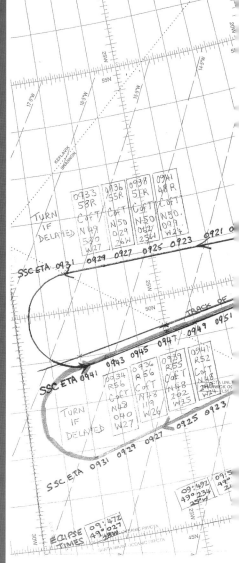

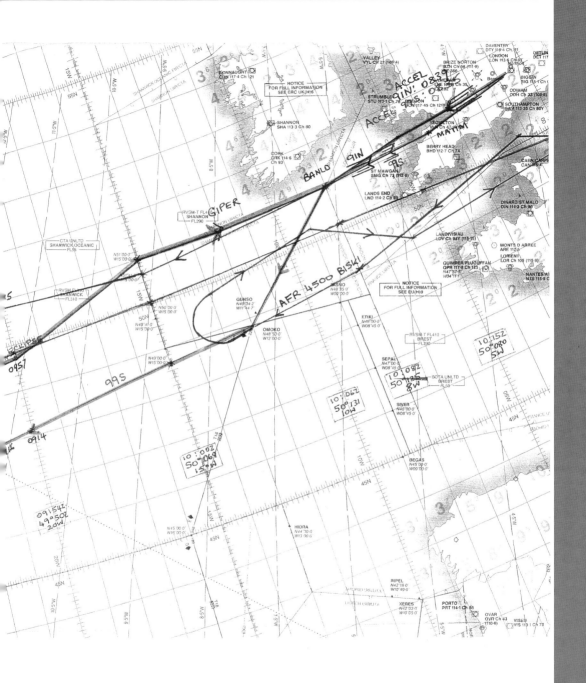

passenger windows on the starboard side? On the 1973 flight there had only been seven scientists and the flight crew on board, but the proposed Goodwood charter flights would be carrying 100 passengers each. For everyone to see the eclipse, equipped with suitable solar viewing glasses, it would be necessary for the passengers seated four-abreast to change seats in flight, to be seated at the starboard window during the time of totality. With an estimated possible eight minutes of totality this was felt to be feasible.

On the 1973 exercise there had been only one Concorde in the air; the present plan was for British Airways to fly two and Air France also decided to fly one of their Concordes. So now we had to discuss not only the logistical problem, but also the effect of shock waves on two Concordes flying in close proximity to each other. British Aerospace delved into the shock wave problem, drawing conclusions from previous experience with both Concorde and military aircraft. They felt that if a 4,000ft vertical separation was maintained there would be only momentary interference during the acceleration phase if both aircraft accelerated together.

By this stage I had been asked by Captain Mike Bannister, Flight Manager Concorde, who would be flying one of the BA aircraft, if I would fly the other. Of course, I readily agreed. I linked up with Lucy Pesaro of Navigation Services who was working on flight planning. As the whole operation was time-critical and involved two Concordes operating on the same inbound track to the UK in Shanwick's Oceanic airspace, it was necessary for us to visit Shanwick Control at Prestwick to discuss the logistical problems. My input was needed when it came to what was possible and what was not. In the event our meeting went well and Lucy and I came away with a 'GO' situation.

Lucy did all of the calculations and produced the final plan. It was planned that the two Concordes would depart within 2 minutes of each other and proceed to their normal acceleration point in the Bristol Channel, where the first Concorde would accelerate followed by the second 4 minutes later. Both aircraft would proceed on the same

track to 8W (8 degrees West) where the first Concorde would turn in a south-westerly direction to eventually take up a track out to 28W. The second Concorde would continue on track to 28W. At this point both aircraft would be some 240 nautical miles apart. At 28W the first Concorde would turn right and the second turn left to meet up again at 28W, flying back to the UK on the track of the eclipse. To avoid any embarrassment the first aircraft would fly in the block FL550–FL600 (55,000ft–60,000ft) and the second from FL450–FL510 ensuring that there would be a minimum of 4,000ft separation. Both aircraft would then proceed on the same track to view the eclipse. In the event that a problem arose with the higher Concorde, necessitating a deceleration and descent, it would turn north. Likewise, the lower aircraft inbound would decelerate and descend early. It had become apparent by this time that the Air France Concorde flight plan would not conflict with the BA Concordes.

The theory all sounds very good, but what if the timings changed for whatever reason? Lucy produced a 'how goes it' chart (see diagram) showing the tracks of both the BA Concordes and the Air France aircraft. BA9099C (the flight number of the aircraft flown by Mike Bannister, abbreviated to 99S, taking the southerly route) is marked in red and BA9091 (abbreviated to 91N, taking the northerly route) is marked in blue. Alongside each track can be seen the ideal time for that position in blue numbering and above, in black, the position to turn if delayed together with the centre of the turn and the radius. The normal centre-of-turn and radius was on our navigation log. At the bottom of the chart are printed the eclipse times at various positions. I was given the choice before the actual flight to have either a TV camera crew on the flight deck or to take along Lucy. I elected to take Lucy!

Because of the logistics in despatching two Concordes, a strict plan had to be organised as follows:

Flight	Chocks off	Optimum take-off	Last possible take-off
99S	0715	0800	0820
91N	0735	0802	0820

All times are UTC. If take-off was delayed beyond 0820 the flight(s) would have to be cancelled.

So, with the planning all complete, the wheels were put in motion for the actual flights. Goodwood Travel dealt with all the marketing in their impeccable way and provided the passengers, and British Airways organised the aircraft and crews.

The day dawned and I reported to the British Airways Flight Crew Briefing at Heathrow to complete all the necessary planning and paperwork. My crew for the flight were Co-pilot SFO Rick Reynolds and Flight Engineer SEO Ian Radford. We were allocated G-BOAC for the flight.

In the meantime the passengers were checking in with Goodwood Travel at the Sheraton Skyline Hotel where they were to enjoy a champagne breakfast – speaking to them later I discovered that some were too excited to eat. On each of the flights, in addition to our normal cabin crew, we would be carrying two Goodwood Travel representatives. They had the unenviable task of shepherding their excited guests from the Skyline and getting them seated on the aircraft. Experience in the past had shown that on arriving at the aircraft the majority of passengers on these non-scheduled special flights are eager to photograph the aircraft from all angles. As these eclipse-chasing flights were so time-critical, it was essential that the passengers boarded the aircraft promptly. In addition to stowing their goods and chattels and making themselves comfortable, it was desirable for passengers to have a seat-change practice before departure and for us to brief them in the use of their viewing glasses.

Having completed our paperwork we proceeded to the aircraft to compete our checks prior to departure. Both aircraft had been refuelled to the same amount so that our weights would be similar and therefore our climb performance compatible. The passengers arrived on time and were quickly ushered aboard. We started up G-BOAC and taxied out for departure, making our take-off within the time

constraints – a sporty take-off as we were lighter than our normal trans-Atlantic weight.

Once safely en-route the passengers were given glasses of champagne and visits to the flight deck commenced. It was imperative during our tracking of the eclipse that the cabin should be clear of glasses and all passengers were seated for the viewing so that seat changes could take place.

We accelerated on schedule and then began our climb into the block for our westward run out into the Atlantic. En-route we carefully monitored our progress with the 'how goes it' chart, and as I had been prudent in taking along Lucy on the jump seat we had our own back-up navigator. All went to plan to 28W and we commenced our left turn to pick up the inbound track of the solar eclipse. At the appointed time we were in position and the viewing and seat changing commenced.

Feedback from the passengers was terrific as they all thoroughly enjoyed the experience. Interestingly, sitting on the port side of the aircraft and unable to leave my seat, I was the only person on board not to witness the event! After the excitement of the eclipse the remaining passengers visited the flight deck as we returned to Heathrow. A truly memorable experience for everyone that took part and, yes, the passengers got to take all the photographs they wanted of the Concorde after landing.

My old school motto was 'Semper Altiora Speramus', which if my memory serves me correctly translates to 'Always strive for higher and better things'. By flying Concorde I believe I fulfilled that edict.

ABOVE Passengers wearing their special eclipse viewing glasses celebrate the occasion with glasses of champagne.
John Stillwell/PA Photos

Chapter 6

The Flight Engineer's View

David Macdonald

David Macdonald began his aviation career as an airframe/engine apprentice with British European Airways, leaving to undertake flight engineer training with BOAC in 1961. His first posting was to the de Havilland Comet 4 before moving on to the VC10. Eleven years on the VC10 fleet included three as an Instructor/Examiner and a further three as a Flight Engineer Superintendent (FES). In 1974 he was appointed to the position of FES Concorde with British Airways, until his retirement in 1994.

OPPOSITE Flight Engineer David Macdonald runs through his pre start-up checks. *Jonathan Falconer*

ABOVE Dave Macdonald and Senior First Officer Tony Yule have time to meet a passenger. *David Macdonald*

RIGHT Pre-flight check at the flight engineer's panel. *Jonathan Falconer*

BELOW Alpha Delta awaits a tow to the passenger terminal. *Ian Black*

FROM LONDON TO BARBADOS

There's a change in the air; the flight engineer's wife noticed it first. He swears he's still the same, but she knows that she's losing him, just like last week and the week before. It begins with a search for the worn-out gold and purple bars to slip onto his shirt, continues through gold pen, lucky tie-clip, licence, passport, manuals, toolkit – where's my ID card? A final buff of the shoes and the transformation is almost, but not quite complete.

Two hours later it is. Alpha Charlie wriggles and shakes her body as I cross the tarmac: I know it's only oleos settling with added fuel, but I can take it as a welcome, after all, haven't I always slapped a tactile greeting as I board?

'Thirty two thousand,' I shout up to Ian, on the steps at the refuel panel. Thumbs up, he confirms the load, adding that today's density is 0.79. We measure fuel by weight, in kilograms. From a comprehensive set of tables, a refuelling sheet will be made out showing the gauge readings to expect for each of the thirteen tanks. I note that four hoses are connected, two on each side, but they're small diameter and it takes an age to get to full tanks (approximately 96,000kgs).

External Inspection

With my flight engineer panel set-up complete, it's time to check outside, beginning at the probe at the very front. It's actually the standby source of pitot and static pressure for flight instruments. Much of the outside check is what may be called 'general condition', ie not bent, bashed or buckled. The nose probe looks straight and its cover has been removed. My friends in the hangar always present a good aircraft, but like so much of our work, we cross-check to safeguard the operation and each other.

From a position at the front I can scan round the radome, along the nose underside – all hatches closed; round to the starboard pitot tubes, static plates and incidence vane, vital sensors for airspeed, altitude and angle-of-attack instruments plus numerous control circuits – temperature probe, the one that

measures +130°C...and the ice-detector. What a contrast.

Ground Power Unit positioned and parked okay, the cable amply supported by a lanyard. Nose gear next and first to the tyres: plain ribbed tyres; they would be changed when the centre groove is worn down, after about 80 landings. Don't just look, scrutinise the tyres. It's useful to have a 5-inch screwdriver in your pocket to use as a depth gauge. Busy airports are notorious for metallic debris. Our dispatch team always check tyre pressures again, after tow-over from the hangar. Small screws or bolts can be picked-up and pushed into the tread as the wheel rolls, becoming barely visible. Specifically check steering torque links, steering lock out for towing, ground-lock pin removal and oleo extension, then generally for any signs of hydraulic fluid. Any vents that we pass should be clear with no sign of leakage, all structure undamaged and all hatches latched closed unless servicing is taking place.

From here we'll walk along the wing leading edge, taking time to admire the complexity of the curves and angles. It's difficult to define 'wing-tip', but turning at the outer extremity we

ABOVE Check sensors and strakes for condition – hatches closed. *Ian Black*

LEFT Tyre tread depth and condition is fine; examine closely for cuts. *Ian Black*

FAR LEFT Remove the nose gear ground-lock pin. *David Macdonald*

LEFT Check wing and elevons for damage – buckets at 21°. *Jonathan Falconer*

LEFT Port wing tip, under-wing PCU fairing and static electricity discharge wicks. *David Macdonald*

see the three starboard elevons, drooped under their own weight, having subsided as engines were last shut down and the hydraulic pressure dissipated. The streamlined chord-wise fairings house the PCUs, tandem hydraulic jacks that drive the elevons, obviously no leaks from here. Note the presence of static dischargers at the elevon trailing edges.

Now walking inboard, pause a moment to look up at the fin starboard side, top rudder PCU, rudders offset in the breeze and more static dischargers – then onwards, to be confronted by the full extent of the power plant, black and white. The rear doors, enclosing the hot end made from titanium, buckets at 21°, showing half-moon gaps at top and bottom: just imagine the reheated gas flow ripping through here at 3,000ft per second.

Forwards now – many vents, clear and no drips – and on to the intake. Here one may see the spill door drooped a little; it doesn't matter, it will close after engine start. Notice also that the auxiliary inlets, set into the spill doors, may be at any position between open and shut. 'Aux Inlets' movement is heavily damped, they will be sucked open as engines run up to idle, and blown shut under differential pressure after take-off. Look very carefully at the ramps and around the intake's sharp leading edges, no blemish can be accepted. It is such a simple shape, but each dimension is vital to the control and positioning of shock waves on the lower lip. Stop and wonder at what will happen here, later this morning – it is aerodynamic wizardry. Look up into the 'ramp void', there's a lot of hydraulics in that space.

There's even more at the next stop, the starboard main landing gear. As with the nose, go straight to the tyres. Examine all of the circumference that's available. These were 256mph-rated, cross-plies until 2001. An aircraft tyre isn't designed for cornering and road-holding, the major objectives being an element of shock-absorption and water dispersal to prevent aquaplaning, thus a plain ribbed design. Cross plies have a 26-ply reinforced carcase, approximately ¾-inch thick with nearly ½ inch of tread vulcanised on to it. The tread itself is reinforced with four sacrificial plies moulded-in; they are exposed with wear, lending a slightly dishevelled air. Use

ABOVE Check fin, rudders, tail gear and rear fuselage for condition; PCUs – no leaks; vents and jettison – outlets clear. *Ian Black*

RIGHT The Michelin Air X radial ply tyre is also fitted to the Airbus A380. *David Macdonald*

RIGHT Top, 22.1-inch cross-ply tyre, note five grooves, triple wire beads with very substantial rayon plies building up a robust, stiff sidewall. Bottom, 22.1-inch radial-ply tyre, only four grooves, single-wire bead and lighter, more flexible sidewall. The light area below the tread is multi-layered Kevlar resulting in a stiff crown area with an element of puncture protection. *Piers Macdonald*

the scissors on your Swiss-army knife to trim them – if they're exposed they've done their job. Loss of centre groove is the time for tyre/wheel replacement. A main wheel tyre lasts about 40 landings. Be suspicious of everything, even the tiniest mark on the surface may go deep – check with the screwdriver tip, keeping a picture of tyre X-section in mind. The mandatory tyre pressure 'check and record' will have been logged already, at 232psi.

Check all of the pipe work, on the bogie, up the leg and into the landing gear bay. The large diameter oblique member is actually the telescopic side-stay; it carries the down-lock at the lower end of the barrel – make sure the ground-lock pin is out. Sandwiched between the leg and the small attached door is the shortening mechanism lock; its ground-lock pin should also be out. In about 15 minutes time the checklist will challenge you on these points. The retraction jack is the more slender oblique; it never looks robust enough!

Continuing aft, skirt round the rear baggage loader to the extended after-body that culminates in the tail navigation light and rear beacon. Did you manage to spot the green nav light in the starboard wing leading edge?

Here, on the fuselage port side, there is one large orifice low down, the jettison outlet for the

LEFT **Main gear bay, retraction jack and telescopic sidestay with ground-lock pin.** *David Macdonald*

occasions when fuel has to be dumped, while the pair higher up are fuel tank vents. Further up still, the bottom rudder PCU.

The aircraft's port side is substantially the same as the starboard, with one notable addition. The port inner elevon fairing houses the Emergency Lowering Ram Air Turbine – its ground lock pin should have been removed.

With fuelling completed there are fuel samples to inspect. Each tank has a water drain

FAR LEFT **Check hydraulics all the way up the leg...** *Jonathan Falconer*

LEFT **...and inside the bay.** *Ian Black*

ABOVE One of two refuel hose panels. *Jonathan Falconer*

ABOVE Be ready with a three foot platform for
this job. *Jonathan Falconer*

RIGHT Twin hose
connections each
side – *collecteur de
remplissage* is the
refuel control unit.
David Macdonald

FAR RIGHT Refuelling
station – starboard
wing root. *Jonathan
Falconer*

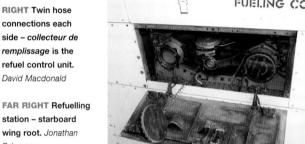

BELOW Refuel panel –
detail. *David Macdonald*

RIGHT Two of the many fuel system water drain
points. *Jonathan Falconer*

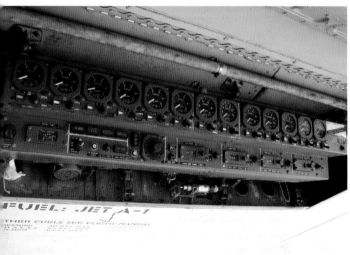

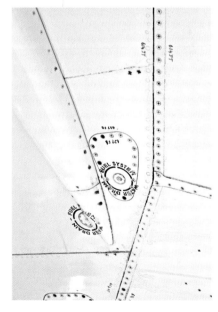

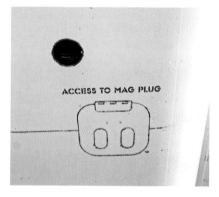

valve at its lowest point. A sample is drawn off
into a glass jar, and water, being heavier than
fuel, sinks to the bottom. Although both are
clear liquids it is easy to see the separation
line. Contents of a jar with no boundary can be
verified with a dab of paste on the end of one's
screwdriver; water changes its colour.

There is a lot to see, a lot to remember, but
knowing the whole aircraft and the way it works
becomes part of the pleasure of going flying.

Twenty minutes to go. It's time to get an
update on Alpha Charlie's recent performance.
Each Heathrow departure and arrival is
attended by a small team drawn from the
group responsible for scheduled maintenance
and defect rectification. They came out of
the hangar and on to the ramp to take-over
refuelling, provide a rapid response to pre-
departure problems and to set up a direct
dialogue between flight and ground crew. This
has been invaluable.

Inside the aircraft the front galley is buzzing

– canapés, champagnes, wines and meals all
to be prepared, all first class and so little time. I
negotiate a pot of tea and a plate of digestives.
Cabin and flight crew are close, we work as one.

I negotiate the 8ft tunnel leading to the flight
deck, stooping ever lower. To the left and right
the main electronic equipment racks, humming
vigorously under the combined effect of five
fans, three pulling and two pushing up to
100lbs of air per minute, drawn from the cabin
and forced through the electronics en-route to
the discharge valves. In the flight deck proper,
headroom is down to 4ft 6in even though there
is 25ft of nose stretching ahead.

Dropping into my chair is like the last piece
of a jigsaw. 'Are you ready, gentlemen?' A mug
of tea in one hand and six pages of Normal
Checklist in the other, the co-pilot calls us to
attention. The ritual litany of the Before Start
Check begins.

The structure and philosophy of the checks,
on the ground, are to prepare the aircraft for the

next phase. After twenty-four items there's a natural 'hold', while load sheet and final payload data are awaited. To obviate a potential source of delay, Load Control will radio the vital figures as soon as the flight is closed. I particularly await Zero Fuel Weight (ZFW), Zero Fuel Centre of Gravity (ZFCG) and the pre-take-off transfer quantity. The first two are inserted into the triple CG computer system, providing amount and disposition of payload. It knows the moment arm of each fuel tank from its program, thus taking instantaneous readings from the contents gauges enables CG to be calculated. Pre-take-off transfer is a calculated amount to transfer from Green Tank 9 (forward) to Green Tank 11 (rear) to adjust laden CG to the take-off value.

This is a good time to check-in with 'Ground'. One of the team will be plugged into the nose-leg intercom point. I've seen the tug arrive, felt it connect a tow bar, but do we have

a start truck connected to each side and are there many bags still to load? Concorde's holds are too small for containers.

This period of increasing tempo has always quickened the pulse, from apprentice days in Heathrow Central to Concorde at Terminal 4: everyone pushing for 'on-time'.

Engine Start-up

I feel each door bang into position; see, on my panel, its warning light extinguish as locks engage. Just the front left, so 'on' with the beacons, letting everyone nearby know that we're about to start. Engine feed pumps 'ON' and a call to Ground – 'when you're clear, pressure on the right for starting three'. An engine revs and on an aircon pressure gauge I see 35psi. There now follows a dialogue, to and fro, between flight engineer (F) and ground engineer (G). It goes something like this:

F *'Here we go, starting 3.'*
Start switch latched at 'START'. Start valve opens, starter turbine spins up and HP spool (N2) begins to rotate; start pump runs. As N2 approaches 10%:

G *'Rotation.'*
He sees LP spool begin to turn.

F *'Fuel on 3.'*
HP valve is set to 'OPEN', admitting fuel to combustion chamber sprayers and switching on ignition. I begin to count in seconds; a good engine should light in about four.

G *'Light-up.'*
Even wearing a full headset he can hear a deep, soft sonorous sound as the vaporised fuel lights. It's followed by a shimmer of heat from the tail pipe.

F *'Confirmed.'*
The exhaust gas temperature (EGT) gauge springs into life, electronic fuel controller modulating flow and rate of EGT rise.

At 25% the engine is self-sustaining, the start valve closes and I operate the 'DEBOW' switch to release the engine to accelerate up to idle. No. 2 engine is started similarly, from a truck connected to the left-hand side.

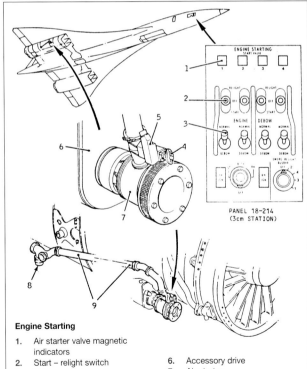

Engine Starting

1. Air starter valve magnetic indicators
2. Start – relight switch
3. Debow switch
4. Manual override knob
5. Air shut-off valve
6. Accessory drive
7. Air starter
8. External air connector
9. Air supply piping

PANEL 18-214
(3cm STATION)

ENGINE STARTING
START VALVE

Each engine actually overshoots idle by about 2 to 3% to clear rotating stall – a phenomenon of flow separation at compressor blades at low engine speeds: going up to a maximum of 72% N2 pops all the little cells, enabling smooth operation thereafter, at all engine speeds. As No. 3 stabilises I reach far to the right to switch on its hydraulic pump, bringing 4,000psi into the Blue system – elevons and rudders snap into line ready for the handling pilot to begin his long and complex Flight Control Check. Remaining hydraulic pumps are set to 'ON'.

With 2 and 3 running, all three hydraulic systems are pressurised; electrical supply is transferred from Ground Power to aircraft generators, all ground equipment is disconnected.

Push-back

'Heathrow Ground', who nowadays sit 283ft up in the air, are masters of the airfield. Nothing moves without their say-so – not even Concorde! With their permission, and clearance from 'Ground', the Captain confirms 'brakes released' and push-back begins.

When working in the noisy environment of an active ramp the phrases 'brakes on' and 'brakes off' are not used – they can sound too alike. 'Brakes release' and 'brakes to park' are preferred.

We leave the start trucks behind, but with 2 and 3 running and their aircon bleed valves and cross-bleed valves open, what would have been an aircon supply can be diverted to 1 and 4's starter turbines for a cross-bleed start.

Engine 4 start follows the same pattern, but this time it is held at half idle rpm (30 to 32%). As soon as it lights, the same process is repeated for No.1. Aircon supply to cabin is reinstated and engines 1 and 4 are held at low rpm until the end of the push-back manoeuvre to minimise towing forces. 'Ground' signs-off with a cheery 'Good-day gents, have a nice flight; pin is on the left.' A nose-gear ground-lock pin had been inserted for push-back, it will be displayed aloft to confirm its removal.

We're on our own.

Taxi

The co-pilot completes the After Start Check and with a 'Your checklist', hands over to

ABOVE Starter hoses connected: ground crew ready for start. *Ian Black*

LEFT Inboard engines running; flight control check underway; ground electrics about to be disconnected; who has forgotten his ear plugs? *Ian Black*

LEFT Towbar being manoeuvered into position at the nose gear. *Ian Black*

the flight engineer. I have my own slim yellow volume ready and open at the Taxy Check page.

'Okay, tug's clear – Nose to 5 and the Taxy Check,' orders the captain.

All of our work is completed over the intercom system, using an ear-defender style headset covering both ears. At a busy airfield like Heathrow there is a constant stream of Air Traffic Control (ATC) exchanges, business-like, succinct, minimalist, perhaps punctuated by a 'Good-day' or a 'Good-morning'. It is a knack, born of practice, to filter out one's own calls at one level, but still hear the sense of everything at another. It's a further knack to weave the call and response Taxy Check seamlessly into the fabric of ATC chatter.

This is a time to sit tall, to look out as well as in. The first five items of Taxy Check concern the pilots and are called and checked. A glance out to see where we are then start the fuel moving. A specific quantity, from the load sheet has been set for transfer. It should give 53%. There follows fifteen items for me alone, read and actioned silently. Alone, but always one of three, never detached. There is a special discipline that enables a flight engineer to perform one function after another with total reliability while still monitoring fuel transfer, always the hydraulics, keeping an eye on brake temperatures and all the while hearing everything coming over the airwaves. The job isn't for everyone. Those who prefer to

concentrate on one job at a time wouldn't like it.

Tank 11 inlet valves snap shut. Good load sheet, pre-take-off transfer produces exactly 53%.

'CG position please.' The two pilots in turn pause at the vertical strip instrument; each replies '53%'.

'Confirmed. Transfer pumps "ON" and Taxy Check complete.'

As we roll onto the runway the ten items of the Before Take-off Check are run. Now is the time to sit small – there is still some residual bounce left in the aircraft despite the new landing gear. A last glance outside, the 2.27 miles of Runway 27L an exercise in perspective. Destination Shannon, Western Ireland, means we're very light, 130 tonnes compared to 185 maximum, nevertheless reheats and full power are still used. This is going to be a sparkling ride, a mustang not a machine.

Take-off Run

'3–2–1–now!' Three thumbs hit three stop clocks, four throttles hit the stops. It takes 7 seconds to spool up to full power, 12 seconds to 100kts, at which point I make a power statement, either 'power checked' or 'engine failure', nothing in between, it's not a conversation.

The countdown? It's not a Hollywood moment, the precise position for noise abatement has been established and, with adjustments for the conditions of the day, calculated back to the start of engine slam to become the 'noise abatement time'. We fly to the half-degree and time actions to the second.

Each engine has a column of five instruments, from the top: N2, N1, Fuel flow, EGT and Area (of the primary nozzle). For a meaningful observation during the 12 seconds one must have a system.

So...see the N2s over 90%; drop down to N1s, all through 81%, the reheat initiation point; drop again to fuel flow catching the reheat annunciator flag and a massive rise from dry engine value; skip the EGTs at this scan – they're moving too fast; drop to Areas, willing them to make that lurch from top-dead-centre to about 4 o'clock, indicating that reheat has lit. Now back to the top, observe N2s stable at 104%, N1s 101%, fuel flow above bugged value, EGTs stable and not above 790 and Areas in the reheated band. There is still time to give a recalcitrant reheat another ignition cycle before 100kts, just!

Rotate

V1, the decision speed, is called. Up to that point I was mentally prepared for a rejected take-off – throttles closed, reverse thrust and brakes. A failure beyond V1 is taken into the air, thoughts now, to that extra bit of power, Contingency Rating, if required. Keep thinking, stay ahead of the game.

'Positive climb. Gear up' is called. Mentally change to scan mode, still on the engines, but take-in gear light sequence (it will take 12 to15

BELOW A stunning shot of reheats and vortex lift at work. *Ian Black*

ABOVE '**Positive
climb. Gear up.**' *Ian
Black*

seconds to complete), airspeed, attitude and
noise timing. Clock lights flash; hunch down,
centre console gripped between knees, right
hand stretched forward onto the throttles, four
left fingers poised over reheat selectors.

'3–2–1–noise!' At the 'n' of noise the
throttles are snapped back to pre-set position
and reheats switched off – undershoot power
by 1% N2 then immediately back, for a good
noise reading. Tip-toe past Windsor; climb
power coming up at 2% per 1,000ft, protecting
Maidenhead and Reading.

Climb to Flight Level (FL) 280, in other words
28,000ft, pick-up Mach 0.95 and 40 minutes
later we're on the ground at Shannon Airport.
Fifty minutes for the passengers to stretch their
legs in duty free.

Shannon Airport

As the last engine whines down to a slow clatter,
I exit promptly, wearing my other hat. Exxon have
connected four hoses already; that was their
brief. This time they're proper 6-inch diameter
man-sized hoses. The refuel control panel is at
the starboard wing root fairing just in front of
the landing gear; the system becomes live as
it is opened. It's not possible to refuel without
electrical power. A line of 13 Fuel Quantity
Indicators (FQIs) dominate, under each one a
switch to open the individual tank refuel valve. As
each tank becomes full a high-level switch will
close it. FQIs are arranged in three groups: 1, 2,

3, 4, 5A, and 7A – these will always be full at any
fuel load; 5, 6, 7 and 8 – the larger wing tanks
that can be preset to shut-off at any level; 9, 10
and 11 – the centre-line, trim transfer tanks that
also have a part-load pre-select.

Refuel

Each pair of hoses couples to a unit that
connects them to the aircraft fuel network. Each
such unit is opened mechanically by a built-in
handle that can also be tripped to 'shut' by
overpressure or overfull electrical signals. It is
particularly sensitive and must be set to open
before there is the slightest pressure applied.
So, with the two units carefully latched open, I
open all thirteen refuel valves and give a 'start
pumping' signal.

The hoses stiffen and roar. It should take
only about 30 minutes at the most to load 80
tonnes of fuel. Exxon pass me the fuel density
and show me the initial sample. I make out my
Refuel Sheet to cross-check individual tank
levels and calculate the expected uplift in litres.

Time now for another external check, this
one quicker than the last, looking for things that
could have occurred during the preceding flight
– chocks away to chocks under. Tyre pressures
have to be checked and recorded again, mains
now up to 260psi as heat soaks through from
the brakes. A quick warm-of-the-hands from
the brake fans and back to the refuel panel
to see the small tanks shut-off at their correct
levels. Now, on with the walk-around, making
full use of the delta to shelter from the rain.

Aer Lingus, resplendent in green oilskins,
arrive with a start truck; we discuss procedure.
At the refuel panel again, I see the rest of the
tanks safely to target levels. Exxon total the
uplift, it matches my calculation – water-check
samples are fine – sign the 'docket' – sign the
Log – a handshake with Exxon and one with Aer
Lingus – one final check of doors and hatches –
exchange hats and...'ready for checks'.

During the transit the co-pilot had deployed
a small printer and a Sharp 1248 loaded with
a load sheet program (remember it's 1987),
every bit as good as the Company mainframe
and with a few useful extras. It was written by a
Concorde flight engineer and approved by CAA.
From it, the co-pilot passes me ZFW and ZFCG
as before; this time we're heavy, full of fuel.

With the numbers inserted, I see that laden CG is 54.2%. For take-off it must be at 54%, thus fuel consumed during taxy will be replaced by a set transfer from the rearmost tank, 11, to 1, 2, 3 and 4. Clearly the forward transfer should not be planned to be more than taxy fuel – that would be silly. (Use of 54% CG for take-off was introduced as a modification after Entry-Into-Service. It is the absolute limit, further aft would compromise nose wheel adhesion.) Taxying today, in the wet, demands a delicate touch and reduced steering angles.

Checks run down to the line, an unmistakeable western Irishman gives start clearance and we all shout 'debow'. A bit of a non-sequitor perhaps, but no-one is going to forget that a warm Olympus 593 has to be run at half-idle speed for one minute, to straighten the HP shaft. While stationary it cools unevenly and bows, hence the term 'debow'. Failure to debow would result in labyrinth seal rub and ultimately high oil consumption.

This sector is what Concorde is all about: 3,791 miles in 3 hours and 32 minutes; V1 = 169kts; Rotate = 192kts; and a maximum performance climb-out.

Back-tracking Runway 24 shows it to be heavily wet. Water ingestion had been a problem on the Concorde prototypes, so the production aircraft sprouted a stirrup-like deflector over the nose wheels to flatten the bow-wave, while a bar across the front of the main wheels breaks up the rooster plume.

Take-off

It's 11.30am and Alpha Charlie wheels round onto runway heading. The Shannon estuary lies 6 miles ahead beyond a fine grey curtain. Perfume drifts on the air as Lesley sashays round my chair, points to the fourth seat; we nod. She pulls forward, buckles up and fixes a headset; very rarely was that seat empty – aah, the good old days!

Throttles to the stops once more. Fifty more tonnes of TOW puts a couple of seconds on to our 0–100 time. Higher weight, higher speed, longer take-off run – just the beginnings of a shake and a plunge as we cross an intersection, but nothing like it used to be.

'Rotate,' calls the co-pilot; the captain nails 13.5° pitch attitude.

'Positive rate-of-climb... gear up.'

Now we're motoring, 270kts maximum until the gear doors are closed. Nose and visor up, reheats off at 500ft, climb power at 1,000ft. I select climb power by throwing a set of ganged switches on the overhead panel, programming electronic units to re-datum TET to the climb schedule; throttles remain on the stops. Get on to the After Take-off Check promptly as the captain aims for VMO – speed and angle-of-attack for optimum aerodynamic efficiency.

VMO is the Maximum Operating speed; it is also the maximum authorised speed and varies with altitude: 300kts at sea level rising linearly to 400kts by 5,000ft; holding 400 until 32,000ft; then linearly again out to 530kts by 44,000ft – holding this speed until it becomes Mach 2 at 50,000ft. This profile defines the high-speed boundary of the flight envelope; it's what we fly at. It is presented on the Air Speed Indicators by a black and yellow-striped pointer, the 'wasp', driven from an Air Data Computer,

The essence of a full performance climb-out is to fly up to the wasp as soon as possible and stay with it – not a couple of knots below, but right on it with the white speed-pointer invisible underneath it! There is a fuel penalty for flying slowly.

Climb-out

With the engines steady at full throttle climb power and the aircraft settled into the 400kts climb we each, quite visibly, relax – straps loosened, seats adjusted. I drop back a couple of notches and swing clockwise, tucking my

BELOW Dave Macdonald at work on the flight deck. *David Macdonald*

feet into behind the co-pilot's chair. Now I can reach everything, from the furthermost hydraulic pump to the throttles and Inertial Navigation Systems (INS).

There are three INS's, all identical and all mounted in the centre console adjacent to each crew position. I follow, and participate in, terminal area and en-route navigation from my set of nav charts, flight log and 'my' INS. If we had been flying overland, to an acceleration point, I would have set No 3 INS to count down the miles-to-go to that point, but here, over the water, we'll hold 400kts passing Mach 1 at about 29,000ft.

Not long to Mach 1, time for a more focussed check of systems; always the hydraulics – how have the contents stabilised after gear, nose and visor retraction? Make a note. AC and DC electrics all okay; cooling, four hard-working, sometimes temperamental, systems will soon be vital; pressurisation about 300ft/min; buckets moving; Secondary Air Doors already checked, with some relief, at 'OPEN'; engine cooling, oil pressure, temperature and contents; intakes ready. Back to the fuel – Red feed tanks on a transfer diet from Tanks 5 and 7 – cross-check the contents by comparison between the addition of all FQIs and the subtraction of fuel used from the start figure. These two numbers are calculated electrically and presented on two readouts.

Unfettered climb performance is very good, even starting at maximum weight. In the USA all aircraft are obliged to fly at 250kts below 10,000ft; for Concorde that's a killer. The wing is so far off-performance; low forward airspeed, but still on climb power results in insufficient ram air cooling to the aircon systems and a sequence of overheat shutdowns and reinstatements.

8,000ft and we're coming up to Mach 0.7, time for the Climb Check, a number of items to be confirmed before 'the acceleration'. Mach 0.7 was chosen as the trigger point since it is at this speed that the first in-flight CG shift takes place, moving from take-off position to 55% by Mach 0.93, thus improving stability at high subsonic Mach numbers.

Tank 11 inlet valves are set to 'OPEN' and Tank 9 pumps switched 'ON', check FQIs' response and CG indication increasing. As Tank

11 becomes full, make sure its inlets close; each of these tanks has an 'OVERFULL' light as a safeguard, but you don't want to be the first to pump fuel overboard through the vent system. As 55% is reached, set 'PUMPS OFF' first, and then close the inlet valves.

As a crew we check through 10,000ft and note CG position, either steady or moving; (same again at 20,000, 30,000, 40,000 and 50,000ft). By 20,000ft we've passed the speed at which most subsonics fly. The co-pilot has negotiated 'accel clearance' from ATC. Air traffic radar controllers know that we need uninterrupted climb and acceleration to Mach 2 at 50,000ft.

Through the Sound Barrier

The 'Transonic Check' is started at Mach 0.93 and is actioned progressively right up to 50,000ft. Just a little way up the road is the 'Sound Barrier', a high drag obstacle stretching between 0.98 and 1.4. Reheats, switched on in symmetric pairs to minimise thrust effect on newly poured drinks, will make light work of it. Reheat operation is timed, maximum run is 15 minutes; it will be used for 10 to 12 minutes on a typical accel. Think speed, think CG; rearward fuel transfer is recommended, still pumping from Tank 9, the flow path being 9 into 5 and 7, into 1, 2, 3, 4 into the engines.

29,000ft, Mach 1, the speed of sound – engaged in October 1947 by Chuck Yeager in the Bell X-1, an air-dropped, rocket-powered aircraft, but probably not fully tamed until Concorde. It could slip by unnoticed, were it not for the cabin displays showing Mach number, altitude, mph and outside air temperature. There is bound to be comment on the lack of sensation as Concorde 'breaks the sound barrier', there always is. All we see, as Mach 1 is passed, is a violent oscillation of static pressure-fed instruments, as a traversing shockwave roars up the static ports. Look at the clock, just 9 minutes from start of take-off roll.

Mach 1.1, check the buckets have reached fully open, now shaping jet efflux for optimum thrust. Approaching Mach 1.3, 36,000ft and 450kts, British Aerospace Guided Weapons territory – the intakes; this is a dual-channel automatic system with a manual inching reversion referenced to an Intake Pressure Ratio gauge (IPR), basically a means of matching intake configuration to engine demand. It pays to watch the intake start-up and operation carefully; you will have to sort it out one day.

There is a definite 'start-up' moment as the ramps make a small angular movement, teasing the shockwaves towards the lower lip, followed by a rapid deployment catching the shocks and holding their origin just in front of the lower lip. The IPR gauges convulse then stabilise at a top-dead-centre position – perfect.

On the fuel panel Tank 9 becomes empty, now there's 12 tonnes in Tank 10 to shift, to drive CG to supercruise position: flow path, 10 into 5 and 7, into 1, 2, 3 and 4.

Mach 1.5 (about 1,000mph) has no special significance to the operation, but it's an interesting number. I expect someone, somewhere, has called it a 'barrier'. Blink and you miss it.

Mach 1.7, off with the reheats, they've done their job. It's good to see the fuel flow drop by about 35% to dry engine value. Here, at 42,000ft we are at the point of maximum airspeed, 530kts; it will be held until it becomes Mach 2 at 50,000ft. Everything is beginning to warm-up – structure, windows, and systems. Soon engine oil contents and hydraulic oil contents will begin to expand – one hopes. The first sign of high oil consumption is a quantity that doesn't expand!

44,000ft and fuel tank vents are closed to allow tanks to be lightly pressurised at 1.2 to 1.5psi, to prevent evaporation losses.

We're pretty well on our own now, in terms of air traffic. When it comes to the cruise segment of flight we are cleared to operate between 50,000ft and 60,000ft for a cruise-climb; allowing the aircraft to gradually drift upwards as weight reduces with fuel consumption.

Finally, at Mach 2, twice the speed of sound, the actual mph varies with temperature, but currently it's 1,320mph. A further set of ganged switches on the overhead panel set the engines to cruise rating, N2 reducing about ½%, TET re-datumed (EGT down to about 670°C), but throttles still on the stops.

It's now 23 minutes from start of take-off, not bad for a 100-seater. The wing has regained its efficiency (after the high drag

ABOVE Pressurise the fuel tanks to prevent evaporation loss.
Jonathan Falconer

zone), CG is at 59% having travelled almost 5ft and intakes, engine and nozzles together produce an amazingly high thermal efficiency. Outside the temperature is –55°C, but the nose structure is up to +120°C. That small piece of uncovered window frame is now much too hot to touch.

I see Tank 10 becoming empty, end of fuel transfer. The very outboard tanks are in the thinnest part of the wing; each holds 2¼ tonnes and while it would be useful to CG to keep them full, their high surface to volume ratio would mean very hot fuel, therefore at this point Tank 5A is transferred into 5, and 7A into 7. It results in a bit of a forward CG creep. To obviate this and maintain a nominal 59% CG, I begin a process that brings 'forward feed tanks' 1 and 4 down from 4,250kgs to 2,000kgs.

Because I'm balancing the aircraft, effectively trimming it, I transfer attention to the 'Icovol' – the finely-calibrated flight control position indicator. The objective is to position the six elevons all in a line and all ½° drooped; this is the minimum drag setting for Mach 2 flight and like every other aspect of the operation it is performed precisely. Each operating pair of tanks, 5 and 7 and 6 and 8 is not symmetric. They have irregular shapes and different contents and moment arms. Thus, with normal fuel usage the aircraft will go out of balance, by varying amounts, in one direction then the other. This trend is picked up from the Icovol and compensated for before it develops, by transferring 200kgs or so from 'heavy' wing to 'light' wing. Elevon trim becomes a routine part of one's scan.

Flight Engineer Training for Concorde –
Pete Phillips, Concorde Flight Engineer, 1976–1999

ABOVE Pete Phillips, pictured when he was flight engineering on the Dutch Lockheed L749 Constellation, PH-LDF 'Flevoland', in September 2002.
Pete Phillips

Pete Phillips joined the Concorde fleet from VC10s in 1976. He had been a CAA-approved examiner/instructor on that fleet and was posted to Concorde to continue that work. He retired in 1999 after 23 years on Concorde. During this period, as well as his line flying, he would have trained all subsequent Concorde flight engineers, conducted the CAA competency checks and constructed and delivered technical refresher courses for both pilots and flight engineers.

Concorde is operated by a three-man flight crew – sometimes two men and one woman, but always two pilots and a flight engineer. A professional flight engineer, trained and experienced as a ground engineer, able to bring a good depth of technical knowledge to the flight deck. His input to Concorde's operation covered a broad spectrum – operation of engines and systems from his station, participation in the general operation and navigation of the aircraft, running the Normal and Emergency Check List procedures and, when required, carrying out ground checks, refuelling and defect rectification. However, one must not forget that in the cramped quarters of the Concorde flight deck one of his most important functions was to pour the tea!

All our flight engineers were experienced on other aircraft types, usually VC10 or 707, but some had logged time on Constellations and one could even speak of flying boats. With the introduction of jet airliners in the 1960s, the job began to

change. The flight engineer took exams in meteorology, navigation, flight planning and R/T (radio licence), formalising his role within an integrated crew. Such teamwork and cross-monitoring was essential to managing Concorde's expanded flight envelope, high performance levels and technical innovation, particularly matching CG fuel trim to speed.

A flight engineer converting onto Concorde would face the longest course in civil aviation, approximately six months in all; so much about the aircraft and its operation was new. From the beginning he would be teamed-up with a captain and co-pilot and they would progress as a unit, through the classroom phase and onto the flight simulator, a programme of eighteen four-hour details covering normal and emergency operation. From this stage onwards training would be conducted by the Fleet's own flight engineer instructors – flight engineers in their own right but also CAA approved instructor/examiners. It was similar for pilots. It was very much a total crew function, with joint briefings and all three 'pupils' expected to understand everything. Woe betides a pilot who drifted off during a flight engineer question; it could be transferred to him rapidly, and vice versa.

By the end of these sessions the crew would have worked through every emergency in the book, from engine failure on take-off, to four-engine flame-out at Mach 2, to major system losses, plus some teasers like 'how to decelerate an aircraft with a fixed intake and failed instruments', and 'how to bring the CG safely down through the corridor without CG position indication'. One of the favourite details was 'incapacitation', when co-pilot and flight engineer changed seats, with the flight engineer being required to bring the aircraft down from Mach 2 to landing, using autopilot, or by hand-flying.

Base flying followed which was the first chance to meet the real aircraft. Principally 'circuits and bumps' for pilots' landings. For the flight engineer it was the first opportunity to get to know the aircraft, the real pace of the operation and to work through the practical element of his training – refuelling, component changes, wheel changes, oiling, etc.

At some point there was still a three-week 'nuts and bolts' course to be undertaken whereby the flight engineers on their own would return to the classroom for a more in-depth technical session.

Finally, a flight engineer was released to the route to operate service aircraft under the supervision of an instructor. Up to twelve flights were undertaken to show him that you were ready to operate on your own as part of a normal crew. With that last box ticked, it was a fantastic feeling to get back to one's natural element after so many months of having every action observed and commented on by an instructor.

But it's never the end. After three months the newly qualified flight engineer is recalled for a competency check on the simulator and then, along with pilot colleagues, settles into the routine of a two-day, latterly three-day, simulator check every six months of his working life. For good measure the flight engineer alone (on a one-to-one basis every 6 months) enjoyed a day of oral questioning to test his technical knowledge of the aircraft. It also included a visit to the hangar to refresh him on some of his ground engineering responsibilities – even a task as ignoble as how to drain Concorde's toilets, so you can see that it was not all roses!

(Quite true. It is known to the authors that this contributor had to devise a method of emptying rather full toilets in the absence of a 'honey cart', while on the ground at Tashkent. What Concorde was doing in Tashkent is another story!)

So, was it worth all the effort? Well, I still have to find anyone who did not enjoy being a flight engineer on Concorde. I believe this was due to the fact that she had to be operated so precisely in order to get the best out of her, and that very few flights were completed without some problem – weather, the aircraft itself or perhaps Air Traffic Control congestion. In an age of ever increasing automation Concorde still required a very high level of crew input, which was rewarding to pilots and flight engineer alike. This reliance on each other resulted in a fantastic esprit-de-corps among the crews that still lasts to this day.

Next waypoint up is 20° West, then pretty much direct to Barbados, slipping past the Azores to the north at 30° West, into the tropics at 50° West. Checks to assess fuel on board at destination are made at each 10° of longitude. Weather reports and forecasts for potential en-route diversions, destination and destination alternates are routinely garnered by the flight engineer from HF or VHF radio sources. The Sharp 1248-assisted engine performance analysis (see 'Engine Health Monitoring') is conducted at intervals, during stable conditions.

18° North and 52° West. Alpha Charlie hits her operational ceiling at 60,000ft; the end of the cruise-climb and the beginning of a conventional constant height, constant speed cruise – if Mach 2 can ever be called 'conventional'.

Descent

At 300 miles out, it's now time to think about deceleration. Loathe as we are to relinquish supercruise efficiency, dropping a boom on the coast is a hanging offence! Today, a decel initiated at 200 miles from Barbados airfield should make us subsonic by the Mach 1 point, 50 miles off the north-east point.

Exactly at 'decel point' the throttles are eased gently back to 18° as bugged on the throttle quadrant. As soon as N2s respond, I transfer attention to the intakes. It's a critical period – ramps lower to the limit of their authority as engine demand reduces. With yet more thrust to come off, the spill door in the

BELOW **Lining-up at Antigua – 10 May 1985.** *David Macdonald*

floor of each intake opens for the first time to dump excess air. Even with such delicate handling, the deceleration effect is felt by all. Think speed, think CG. Next item on the Decel Check initiates a forward CG shift to match CP movement. Fuel path – Tank 11 into 5, and 7 into 1, 2, 3 and 4. Throttle lever angle of 18° is governed by intake capability; idle power could be taken, but mild pop-surging would occur.

At 350kts we begin a descent: at Mach 1.5 a further power reduction, still not idle as we seek to preserve bleed-air mass flow for equipment cooling. As Mach 1.3 approaches, intake surfaces are reset to subsonic mode, ramps fully up and spill doors checked closed. Distance out looks fine and Concorde 273 transitions to subsonic at 35,000ft. Grantley Adams, the Barbados airport, co-ordinates our descent, a North Point arrival, to fly down the west coast where Bridgetown and all the tourist hotels are located.

At 15,000ft, Alpha Charlie bursts through a layer of fair-weather cumulus cloud. Just 3¼hrs after a bleak, rain-swept Shannon, 21 miles of surf-fringed Barbados basks before us – magic!

Speed reduction to 250kts begins and the Approach Check is run. Passage through 270kts is the prompt to lower the visor and set the nose to 5°.

Tracking down the west coast, speed is reduced to 210kts. Running past Bridgetown, field in sight – back to 190kts, all speeds dialled into the auto throttle system. Left-turn onto finals and at 8 miles out the Landing Check.

Approach

Landing-gear is lowered – 4 greens; nose is set fully down at 12.5°. I raise my seat, fully up. With my head bumping the overhead panel I can just keep the runway in sight. I focus on the radio altimeter – I'm going to be calling heights from it – but my scan takes in engines and airspeed.

'1,000ft radio' always seems to change the atmosphere.

The co-pilot responds: '5 greens (4 gear and 1 nose), go-around height set.'

'800ft' and auto throttles are set to final approach speed, 164kts.

'500ft.' Speed is stabilised, angle-of-attack at 14° with throttles moving up to hold speed.

Co-pilot confirms, 'Stabilised'.

ABOVE A superb image of landing attitude at the first kiss of the runway, just before tyre smoke is whipped round in the decaying vortices. Note plenty of up-elevon to combat ground effect. *Ian Black*

'400, 300 ('decision height' – 'continuing'), 200, 100, 50, 40 (auto throttles out), 30, 20, 15.'

Landing

At 15ft radio the aircraft is sitting in 'ground effect' and on the vertical component of thrust, the throttles are eased back to idle and she settles gently onto the runway. The main wheels land and tyre smoke is whipped round by decaying vortices. Engines are set to reverse idle and the nose wheel is landed. With the stick pushed firmly forward to hold the nose wheel on, reverse power is applied. Eight carbon fibre brakes and four reversers create a substantial and reassuring stopping power.

Two engines are shut-down for taxy-in and 4,000kgs of fuel transferred forward into Tank 9 – now, no matter how Alpha Charlie is unloaded, she will never tip. Ground power on – engines off – and it's still only 11.20am. Magic!

LEFT 'The office' – 1969 to 2003. *Ian Black*

BELOW 'The office' – 2005 to...The Airbus A380 flight deck. *Airbus*

Chapter 7

The Ground Engineer's View

Concorde was not an easy aeroplane to work on, everything was compact – from easing a replacement engine between the nacelle walls and the jet pipe, to chasing a wiring snag inside a fuel tank – it was tight. You had to be flexible and not bothered by claustrophobia. Concorde was definitely the sort of project that fostered a loyalty – once you'd started you wanted to see it through, whether you were selling tickets, meeting passengers, in the cabin, on the flight-deck – or keeping it flying, as John Dunlevy and Carl Percey did.

OPPOSITE Alpha Golf is prepared for her final departure from Heathrow to New York, en-route to Seattle, 3 November 2003. *Ian Black*

John Dunlevy, flight-test and avionics engineer, 1965–2003

ABOVE John Dunlevy stands beside Concorde's famous Marilake display panel. *John Dunlevy*

John Dunlevy began his career in 1965 as a Bristol Aeroplane Company apprentice, working and training on 002's flight-test instrumentation, the wind tunnel, and in the drawing office. Upon completion of his apprenticeship he transferred to the Fairford Flight Test Centre where he was concerned with intake development and trials at Fairford and in Casablanca; cold weather and icing trials at Moses Lake, Washington, and endurance flying. He joined British Airways' Concorde Maintenance team on the conclusion of the flight-test period, where he remained until Concorde was withdrawn from service in 2003 – then he retired. He was on the final Concorde flight when AF and John 'came home' to Filton. If he isn't the only man in the world to have spent his whole working life on nothing but Concorde, then he will be one of a very small number!

Carl Percey, licensed aircraft engineer, 1968–to date

BELOW Carl Percey at the refuel panel. *Carl Percey*

Carl Percey started his tool-making apprenticeship with BAC at Weybridge in 1968. During that period and for four years afterwards he worked on the production and assembly of Concorde's forward fuselage and tail cone. From there he joined the British Airways' Concorde Maintenance Team in 1976, staying with the aircraft until its withdrawal from service in 2003. He has worked on the Concorde project for 34 years, plus volunteer time on the reassembly of aircraft 202, G-BBDG, at Brooklands. He currently works for British Airways on Boeing 747 and 777 maintenance.

Both have worked on Concorde, man and boy, for over 30 years – Carl 34 years and John 38 years. Both took apprenticeships in the industry: John followed the electronics/avionics discipline at the Bristol Aeroplane Company, which became part of the British Aircraft Corporation (BAC), then British Aerospace (BAe) and finally BAe Systems. Carl's experience was in the mechanical field, a toolmaker and structures man at BAC Weybridge (formerly Vickers), becoming airframe/engine qualified at British Airways. Between them they have 72 years of Concorde experience – not counting rebuilding Delta Golf at Brooklands!

Like any piece of any complex machinery Concorde had a planned maintenance programme and there were two distinct teams

to handle it, Majors and Minors: nothing to do with age, experience or skill!

Very early on in Concorde's service life it was realised that the aircraft needed a different approach to how we worked with other groups. It was agreed that we come out of the hangar and on to the ramp for every Concorde movement. We bagged a couple of Portakabins adjacent to Concorde's regular gates as our away-base. We took over the refuelling task, a complicated system full of safety circuits; it needed very careful handling. Flight crew would drop in before boarding; they said it

was to discuss that day's service aircraft, but they always stayed for tea. That liaison, both before and after flights, was very good for the project; to be able to discuss any problems face-to-face was much better than just reading log entries. The major benefit, however, was being ready at the aircraft side with manpower and spares should any defect arise during crew checks, start-up and departure. We were on intercom headset during engine start, watching for anything untoward, ready for a manual start if necessary, then waiting on-site listening-in on the radio as the aircraft taxied out, only packing

ABOVE LEFT BA engineering lads with Concorde wheels at Prestwick. *Carl Percey*

ABOVE A foggy morning at Prestwick. *Carl Percey*

LEFT The flames that result from a late light-up. When it does ignite there's lots of highly atomised fuel in the tail pipe which shoots out a flame. It's not damaging in any way, but ATC have to be persuaded not to send out the fire brigade! *Carl Percey*

our kit to return to the maintenance area after the flight engineer called us on 'Concorde Tech' company radio to say that they were safely airborne and no problems.

The arrival of an incoming Concorde would start with the workforce gathered around the radio, waiting for the aircraft to call in with an estimated time of arrival and a list of any problems so that parts could be ordered in advance. One person would drive out to the arrival ramp to make a tarmac inspection, looking for any sharp or hard objects, especially in the path of wheels and engines. As the aircraft parks, the headset man confirms 'chocks in position' and ground power available. When all wheels are chocked fore and aft he will request brakes to be released, to permit cooling air to circulate through the discs.

The brake fan exhausts are checked at this point – all should be blowing warm air; a cold flow indicates an inoperative brake.

Time now for a crew debrief, an opportunity to discuss any snags in depth. Particularly valuable is to know when and where any fault arose – was it a 'hard' fault or intermittent? The worst sort was those that happened in supercruise, but disappeared as the aircraft decelerated and cooled in subsonic flight.

Next, another thorough examination of the aircraft exterior, a tyre pressure and brake wear check, engine oils and IDG oils checked, hydraulic contents topped up to 5.0, 6.9 and 3.1 US gallons for Green, Yellow and Blue systems respectively. Note that main gear tyre pressures could be up to 260psi due to heat radiating through from the brakes; don't deflate

down to the normal 232psi as their pressures would reduce once cooled.

There were only occasional periods when we did a 'tarmac turn-round', when the aircraft went straight out again on another service. The minimum maintenance and refuel time for this would have been two hours. Departure times were pitched for passenger needs, so usually the aircraft would have to vacate the gate and be towed back to HQ.

At the hangar we would know from the Maintenance Control department whether the aircraft would be a 'runner' for the next day's flights, or if it was scheduled for planned maintenance. This is where the two teams come in.

We have four levels of maintenance checks, beginning with the basic preparation-for-flight Ramp Check; next is the Service Check, which is scheduled at every 175 flying hours and is a two-day procedure; it is followed by the Inter Check at 1,100 flying hours – approximately an annual event; and finally the Major Check at 12,000 flying hours.

The Minor Maintenance Team looks after flight preparation, the Service Check and will carry out all defect rectification on incoming aircraft and will assist with Inter Checks as required. The Major Maintenance Team is responsible for the Major Checks and Inter Checks.

In addition to the items already covered, a Ramp Check would also require a check of all illuminations and warning lights, cabin signs and emergency lights, navigation, landing and anti-collision lights. The multi-track flight recorder would be replaced after every flight for routine reading. This is not the orange-coloured 'black box' recorder so popular with the press: that one is located on an electronic rack by the rear galley, along with the cockpit voice recorder.

The two battery volts/amps and acid levels are checked and the battery replaced every three months; they are, after all, the last-ditch source of electricity and must last for at least 15 minutes in an emergency. Note that Alpha Golf has nickel/cadmium batteries. Every 30 hours the engine nacelle doors must be opened up to carry out a tightness check on all oil, hydraulic and electrical couplings – there is an inherent aerodynamic/acoustic vibration at the rear, but the passengers don't feel it.

Every 50 hours engine oil samples are drawn off for laboratory analysis as part of the engine health monitoring process. We are looking not so much for visible metallic particles but the microscopic, measured in parts per million.

The Service Check at 175 hours is a little more in depth. At this check, hydraulic oil samples are sent for analysis. Engine oil scavenge filters are removed and sent for

BELOW Alpha Foxtrot in the hangars at Heathrow for a Service Check. *John Dunlevy*

appraisal; new ones are fitted. We all remember that the engine scavenge filters are double units, a filter within a filter; one that looks clean on the outside may have debris trapped in the inter-space. Magnetic Chip Detectors are removed and any 'sludge' collected. A full oil-change may be called-up. Heat shielding and insulation around the engines is inspected; the cabin floor is lifted to inspect the under-floor fuselage fuel tank area.

Whereas the first two stages of the engine compressor can be examined by crawling into the intake, and the LP turbine and reheat assembly checked from within the jet pipe, the rest of the engine is viewed by borescope – the medical people have the same kit, but call it endoscope. There are blanked-off ports

at strategic locations throughout the engine, designed to take the miniaturised viewer, giving us either a direct view through the eyepiece or a larger picture on a portable screen; most of us prefer the clarity of the direct view. By these means we can see all stages of compressor, the combustion chamber and its vaporisers, the turbines and their nozzle guide vanes. Borescope checks have both routine call-up and specific engine monitoring programmes. At one point we boroscoped the combustion chambers at every London visit; it saved millions of pounds in the long term as damage can be intercepted while it is still at the deterioration stage. We're looking for any foreign object damage through the compressor stack; small splits, tears, erosion, damaged vaporisers in the

combustion chamber; cracks, nicks or burning at the turbine end.

The Maintenance Manual carries all details of permissible damage and the limits beyond which the engine must be changed. An engine change will be handled by our Minor Maintenance Team: we would complete the task, including an engine run, within one 8-hour shift using 6 men – 4 airframe/engine and 2 avionics.

The engine is secured by 6 mounting bolts – 4 main with nuts torqued to 1,950ft lbs and the 2 forward sets torqued to 475ft lbs. All accessory system and control couplings are released and a Sabena hoist is placed on top of the wing. The hoist's two cables are attached to the engine then the jet pipe is separated from the engine to provide about half an inch of clearance – that's all there is. When everyone is ready the hoist takes the strain, the six mounting bolts are removed and the engine is lowered onto a purpose-built trolley. Installation is pretty much a reverse of that process. A specific check-out engine run is completed in the run-up bay and oil filters are examined. A very full day's work.

The Inter Check is altogether different. It can take anything from one to three weeks to complete. There is a series of Inter Checks – 1, 2, 3 etc, each one concentrating on a particular zone, accomplishing deep inspections to structure, hydraulics, fuel, electrical cabling and components. The findings will become part of the aircraft's 'life extension' dossier. The aircraft is jacked in readiness for a gear swing – landing gear retractions and extensions. Many routine component changes will be called-up. At some point during this check sequence all four engines will be dropped to facilitate cable inspection: this will be one of the longer checks, because heat from an SST's engine

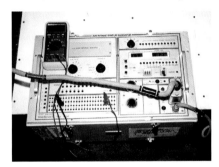

operating at Mach 2 for hours on end will
harden insulation, even though it is specially
made for Concorde. Fuel tanks will be drained
and opened up for minor defects of wiring
and sealant to be fixed. Again, Concorde has
a special Viton tank sealant, but the heat still
hardens it and the expansion and contraction
of the structure can cause small splits. This is
a very difficult job – small access panels and a
thin wing. The tank has to be vented for at least
24 hours beforehand, and when new sealant is
applied it must be left to cure for 48 hours. Full
access to tanks 5A and 7A in the outermost
part of the wing is impossible. We've developed
a technique to get around this: one end of a
hollow tube is taped to one's index finger and
the other (top) end taped to your arm. A syringe
is then inserted into the top end and the sealant
is squeezed down the tube and into the fuel
tank where it is applied by index finger using
feel or touch.

The longest Inter Checks of all usually have
high modifications content – the manufacturer
develops modifications, some of them
mandatory, and agrees a programme with the
airlines, while the authority (CAA) states an
end-date for full fleet implementation. Systems
checks after such work are very substantial.

They are even more so following the Major
Check. This is a three-month full investigation
of the whole aircraft, with such structural work
as is required taking precedence. It would not
be unusual to replace all nacelle cabling and
connectors and similarly throughout the intakes.
The whole period culminates with a paint strip,
chemical cleaning, respray and a return to
service in an 'as new' condition.

The Concorde years have been an
engineering and maintenance challenge.
Twenty-seven years in service – we must have
got most of it right.

12,000-hour Major Check

ABOVE Concorde undergoes a Major Service inside British Airways' Technical Block B at Heathrow. *John Dunlevy*

RIGHT Flight instrumentation is removed from the aircraft to facilitate the work of the maintenance engineers. *John Dunlevy*

RIGHT The stripped-out interior with mid-fuselage passenger cabin bulkhead in the foreground. *John Dunlevy*

ABOVE The droop nose and nose cone. *John Dunlevy*

ABOVE Internal wiring looms above the flightdeck tunnel. *John Dunlevy*

LEFT The tail section looking forward. To the left is the vertical stabiliser minus its two rudders. *John Dunlevy*

ABOVE Port wing stripped of its paint and fittings, elevons and engines. *John Dunlevy*

BELOW Its Major completed, Concorde is towed to the paint shop for respraying. *Carl Percey*

Appendices

{"image_fulltext": ""}

OPPOSITE **Rolls-Royce Olympus 593-610 first stage low pressure compressor blades.** *David Macdonald*

Appendix 1

Surviving Concordes

Prototypes and pre-production aircraft

F-WTSS (001)
**Air and Space Museum
(Musée de l'Air et de l'Espace),
Paris, France**
Aéroport de Paris-Le Bourget,
Boite Postale 173 Paris, France
Tel: 00 33 1 49 92 71 99
www.mae.org

G-BSST (002)
**Fleet Air Arm Museum,
Yeovilton, Somerset,
England**
RNAS Yeovilton
Ilchester
Somerset
BA22 8HT
Tel: 01935 840565
www.fleetairarm.com

G-AXDN (101)
**Imperial War Museum, Duxford,
Cambridgeshire, England**
Duxford Airfield
Cambridgeshire
CB22 4QR
01223 835000
www.duxford.iwm.org.uk

F-WTSA (102)
**Musee Delta Athis-Paray Aviation, Orly
Airport, Paris, France**
40 av Jean Pierre Bénard
91200 Athis Mons
France
Tel: 01 69 38 83 38 / 01 60 48 14 48
www.museedelta.free.fr

F-WTSB (201) and F-BVFC
**Airbus France, Toulouse-Blagnac,
France**
Site de Saint Martin du Touch
316 route de Bayonne
31060 Toulouse Cedex 9
France
Tel: 00 33 5 61 93 55 55
www.stagev4.airbus.com

G-BBDG (202)
**Brooklands Museum, Weybridge, Surrey,
England**
Brooklands Museum
Weybridge
Surrey KT13 0QN
England
Tel: 01932 857381 ext 221
www.brooklandsconcorde.com

Production aircraft

G-BOAA
National Museum of Flight, East Fortune, Scotland
East Fortune Airfield
East Lothian EH39 5LF
Scotland
Tel: 0131 247 4238
www.nms.ac.uk

G-BOAB
London-Heathrow Airport, England
In storage.

G-BOAC
Manchester Airport Aviation Viewing Park, England
The Aviation Viewing Park, Sunbank Lane
Altrincham WA15 8XQ
England
Tel: 0161 489 3932
www.manchesterairport.co.uk

G-BOAD
Intrepid Sea Air & Space Museum, New York, USA
Pier 86, W 46th St and 12th Ave
New York, NY 10036-4103
USA
Tel: 001 646 381 5010
www.intrepidmuseum.org

G-BOAE
Grantley Adams International Airport, Barbados
Barbados Concorde Experience
Grantley Adams International Airport
Christ Church
Barbados
Tel: (246) 420 7738
E-mail: info@barbadosconcorde.com

G-BOAF
Concorde at Filton, Bristol, England
Airbus UK main factory site
Southmead Road
Bristol BS34 7RG
England
Tel: 0117 936 5485
www.concordeatfilton.org.uk

G-BOAG
The Museum of Flight, Seattle, USA
9404 East Marginal Way S
Seattle, WA 98108-4097, USA
Tel: 001 206 764 5720
www.museumofflight.org/concorde

F-BTSD
Air and Space Museum (Musée de l'Air et de l'Espace), Paris, France
Aéroport de Paris-Le Bourget,
Boite Postale 173 Paris, France
Tel: 00 33 1 49 92 71 99
www.mae.org

F-BVFA
Smithsonian National Air and Space Museum, Washington DC, USA
Boeing Aviation Hangar
Steven F. Udvar-Hazy Center
14390 Air and Space Museum Parkway
Chantilly, VA 20151, USA
Tel: 001 202 633 1000
www.nasm.si.edu

F-BVFB
Auto & Technik Museum Sinsheim, Germany
Museumsplatz, D-74889 Sinsheim, Germany
Tel: 00 49 (0) 7261/9299 0
www.sinsheim.technik-museum.de

F-BVFF
Paris-Charles de Gaulle Airport, Paris, France
On display alongside taxiway.

Appendix 2

Units of measurement

A viation is perfectly at ease with a variety of units. Ask of any Concorde pilot his weather limits for automatic landing and he will reply, without any trace of whimsy, '15 feet decision height and 250 metres runway visual range'. Whatever the perceived anomaly or deviation from SI units (*Système International Unites*), there is always a reason.

Take weight as a prime example. By the late 1950s operators worldwide were moving to kilograms, but each Concorde revision continued to be defined by a take-off weight expressed in thousands of pounds. Even the final version delivered to Air France and British Airways had a maximum taxi weight of 412,000lbs, take-off weight of 408,000lbs

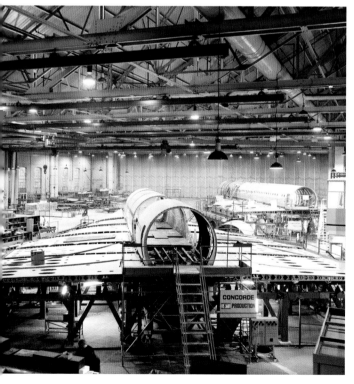

and landing weight of 245,000lbs, translating to 186,880kgs, 185,070kgs and 111,130kgs respectively. Why? It was expected of Air France and BOAC (British Airways) to buy – to showcase – but the important market penetration was always the USA, who, still to this date, works in pounds.

(Note that the round number, Fuel Saving Landing maximum of 130,000kgs was a post-EIS British Airways request.)

Systems were blessed with a mixture of units, partly political and partly pragmatic. It was agreed that pressure would be measured in pounds per square inch throughout, thus pressurisation air was bled from the engine at 65psi, but its flow measured in kgs/sec.

Likewise, engine oil pressure was shown in psi, but the oil quantity gauge calibrated in US quarts (4 quarts = 1 gallon). And the hydraulic systems followed a similar pattern, with contents gauges registering in US gallons.

In these latter two cases the oils in question could be purchased only in US quart cans, US gallon cans and 55 US gallon drums. (1US gallon = 0.833 Imperial gallons = 3.785 litres).

This leaves just the linear measurement case. Principal aircraft dimensions have always been stated primarily in feet and inches. The UK industry adopted metres during the 1960s, hence Heathrow's longest runway at 12,800ft became 3,902 metres and Concorde's horizontal visibility limit was established at 250 metres. However, in the vertical sense, we have the tried and tested, near-worldwide system of Flight Altitudes and Flight Levels generally expressed in whole number thousands of feet, affording both good traffic flow capacity and safe levels of aircraft separation. China, North Korea and much of what was the USSR use metric flight levels set at 300-metre intervals – a clumsier system, unlikely to become standard.

Thus to enunciate '15 feet and 250 metres' in the same breath may sound odd, but there is good logic.

Appendix 3
Glossary

ADF	Automatic Direction Finding
ADS	Air Data System
AFCS	Automatic Flight Control System
APU	Auxiliary Power Unit
ASI	Airspeed Indicator
ATC	Air Traffic Control

Boundary Layer
The layer of air extending from the surface of the object to the point where no dragging effect is discernible

C of A	Certificate of Airworthiness
C of G	Centre of Gravity
C of P	Centre of Pressure, the point at which the sum of all lifting forces on a wing can be said to act
Chord	The measurement from the leading edge of a wing to the trailing edge

Delco	Inertial navigation used by British Airways
DME	Distance-Measuring Equipment

EGT	Exhaust Gas Temperature
Elevons	Flight control surfaces combining elevator and aileron

FAA	Federal Aviation Administration

HF	High Frequency radio signals
HP	High-Pressure compressor or turbine

IAS	Indicated Air Speed
ILS	Instrument Landing System
INS	Inertial Navigation System

L/D	Lift/Drag ratio
LP	Low-Pressure compressor or turbine

Mach no (M)
Unit of speed relative to the speed of sound, e.g.: M1.0 = the speed of sound

MTOW	Maximum Take-off Weight

N1/N2	Engine speed relationship
N1	Low pressure compressor speed
N2	High pressure compressor speed
Ogival	The particular convex curved shape of Concorde's wing planform

RAT	Ram-Air Turbine
RTOW	Regulated take-off weight. The maximum take-off weight governed by atmospheric and runway conditions of the day

RF	Radio Frequency
RVR	Runway Visual Range

SNECMA	Société Nationale d'Étude et de Construction de Moteurs
SST	Supersonic Transport
Subcruise	Concorde's subsonic cruise at M 0.95

Supercruise
Concorde's supersonic cruise at M 2.0

TAS	True Airspeed
TET	Turbine Entry Temperature

V1	Take-off decision speed
V2	Take-off safety speed
Vmca	Speed for minimum control in air after engine failure
VOR	VHF Omni-Directional Range
VR	Rotation speed on take-off
Vref	Approach speed, varies with aircraft weight

VSI	Vertical Speed Indicator

Index